TIME

TIMESHARING
The Practical Guide

BRIAN L. WATES

David & Charles
Newton Abbot   London   North Pomfret (Vt)

To Ger and those in the industry
who made this book possible.

British Library Cataloguing in Publication Data

Wates, Brian L.
　Timesharing: the consumer guide.
　1. Vacation homes　2. Timesharing (Real
　estate)
　I. Title
　647'.94　　　　TX303

　ISBN 0–7153–8811–8

Phototypeset in Linotron Futura
by Northern Phototypesetting Company, Bolton
and printed in Great Britain
by A. Wheaton & Company Limited, Exeter
for David & Charles Publishers plc
Brunel House, Newton Abbot, Devon

Published in the United States of America
by David & Charles Inc
North Pomfret, Vermont 05053, USA

Preface

There is no-one more knowledgeable, competent or capable of writing about timesharing than Brian Wates. He has been in this new industry since its inception in the early seventies, and has travelled on business extensively so he knows about multi-ownership both here in this country and in many other parts of the world.

I am delighted to have the opportunity of writing this preface for Brian, since he and I have worked closely together for some six years since the founding of the British Property Timeshare Association, which came into being in no small measure due to Brian's effort and energy.

Knowledge of problems and conditions in the timeshare industry throughout Europe is becoming increasingly important as many prospective British timeshare purchasers are looking to the concept as a means of achieving an annual European vacation. A book of this kind, which is the first-ever consumer publication aimed for the European market, is therefore to be welcomed not only for present timeshare owners but, more particularly, for those contemplating going into timesharing. Indeed the timeshare industry represents the fastest growing sector of the leisure market.

Timesharing will become widespread in view of its ability to provide owners and their families with a hedge against inflation. Similarly, by using property banks and exchange companies, owners are enabled to take their holiday not just in their own property but from a choice of locations on a worldwide basis.

Thus the importance of this consumer-orientated work by Brian Wates.

The Earl of Lindsay
Chairman,
British Property Timeshare Association

December 1986

Contents

8

Foreword

In the autumn of 1971, I advertised in the Sunday Times offering individuals the opportunity to spend a weekend in the Swiss Alps with a view to inspecting and possibly purchasing a timeshare. On our first weekend inspection trip every person purchased, the same held true for our second experience.

It was obvious to me then that timesharing had something going for itself. In 1973, I launched my own timeshare scheme which regretfully was not successful. At the same time I launched Holiday Exchange Club, a vehicle to exchange time in the owners' units. HEC merged with Resort Condominium International in 1977 when I joined the latter as MD for Europe and Africa.

In 1983, I left RCI to form my own company, Tourism Advisory Group, which provides marketing services, statistics and publications to the industry and more recently The Timeshare Bourse, which is now Europe's largest timeshare resale and rental organisation.

During my fifteen years in the industry, I have been fortunate to witness its tremendous explosion from just a trickle of activity in the late sixties/early seventies to now nearly two million owners in fifty-five countries throughout the world.

During the past three years, Great Britain has experienced a tremendous growth both in the development of timeshare resorts and of the British who have purchased. As the industry progressed, it inevitably drew some bad as well as good developers and marketers into it. The effects of under-capitalised and sharp-end operations have led to a recent spate of bad press and general media criticism which has caused many individuals to question the value of the timeshare product.

In *Timesharing*, I have endeavoured to eliminate my own bias and present a detailed framework of just what the industry is all about. After all, timesharing is the fastest growing sector of the world's travel industry so something must be right. I hope this book will unravel the confusion and complexity of the product.

Brian L Wates   Lavenham, Suffolk

Introduction

What is Holiday Timesharing?

Holiday timesharing is one of the biggest innovations in the international leisure industry since the post-war boom in package holidays. A phenomenon of the early 1960s, it has grown by leaps and bounds to stretch right round the world; in fact, at the time of writing it already covers over fifty-five countries. The concept is still evolving, and new variations on the theme continue to be introduced, thereby adding to the breadth of its appeal.

TABLE 1
GROWTH OF TIMESHARING IN UK AND IRELAND

Year	1975	80	81	82	83	84	85	86 (est.)
England		9	12	16	23	28	29	31
Scotland	1	4	5	6	8	10	11	13
Wales		1	1	1	2	2	2	4
Isle of Man						1	1	1
Channel Islands		1	1	1	1	1	1	1
Republic of Ireland		1	2	2	3	3	3	5
Total	1	16	21	26	37	45	47	55

Resorts in existence by end December

TABLE 2
GROWTH OF TIMESHARE OWNERSHIP IN UK AND OVERSEAS
BY BRITISH RESIDENTS

Year	Family Ownership
1975	150
1980	5,000
1981	12,000
1982	17,500
1983	23,000
1984	30,000
1985	50,000
1986 (est.)	85,000

Holiday timesharing, also known as time-ownership or multi-ownership, among other names, means a lifetime of holidays for a once-only payment. Co-ownership programmes tend to be related to resorts which sell in multiples of one week, such as one, two or three months. These are known within the industry as fractional interests (of which more details are given in Chapter 1).

Timesharing, described simply, is a legal arrangement which allows you and your family or friends to acquire the right to use a holiday home for one or more days or weeks each year for a successive number of years. That is to say, you opt for the time of year most convenient to you at the resort of your choosing, which is then yours to use as you wish, and when you go away the arrangement is that it will be well looked after and in perfect condition for your return the following year.

How Does it Work?

There are a variety of holiday timeshare ownership schemes in operation in Great Britain, Europe, and throughout the world. The most common amongst British purchasers is club membership – briefly, you become a member of a club owning rights in the resort. Other schemes entitle you to a freehold interest or an equity (shareholding) interest in your purchase; with others you may acquire a lease or licence to use your chosen apartment, lodge or villa.

The net effect is that the legal structure – where appropriate – divides the building into separate apartments and divides the apartments, or other buildings, into fifty-two separate weeks. Usually, one or two weeks are reserved for the building's annual maintenance and refurbishment.

The remaining fifty weeks are then given fixed dates, either Saturday to Saturday or another convenient day of the week. In some cases, an actual calendar date is allocated to each week, for example 1–7 January, 7–14 January and so forth throughout the year. The individual weeks (unit weeks) are then allocated a sequential number (1–52) or, in some cases, a letter (A, B, C and so on). The rights to unit weeks are then made available to the purchaser for either a fixed number of years, usually twenty-five years or more – with or without residual rights to share in the realisable value of the asset, or in perpetuity. In the latter case you own the rights to occupation for the natural life of the building and a share in the property value should the building be demolished at some future date.

Whatever your occupation rights, your interests are then bound jointly to the other owners under a covenant, which creates a home owners' association and provides the necessary vehicle for the continued management of the building.

For our discussion, let us take a fifty-apartment timeshare building offering fifty unit weeks of timeshare per apartment (two weeks being reserved for maintenance and repairs). This example gives us some 2,500 unit weeks for sale. Therefore, in theory, 2,500 families could own the building or the rights of occupation thereof. In practice, most families will purchase an average of 1.5 unit weeks.

The number of purchases is usually higher for resorts offering what are considered primary holidays, for example Marbella or Florida, and shorter for resorts offering 'second holidays', for example Scotland, the Dordogne or New York's Poconos. Therefore, a more realistic level would on average be 1,670 families. Of course, as an owner, you will only see the normal fifty-apartment building occupied by fifty or so families and not the other 1,620 families. The developer will also ensure your privacy by restricting the occupancy to usually two people per bedroom and living room, the latter of which usually has a convertible sofa.

Our timeshare building is, if we look at it logically, no different from any other building in terms of the number of tenants. Most of us leave our homes every day at least once. The fact that on one day of the week some families leave home and others enter, with an efficient maid service, makes little change in the tempo of the building, except for perhaps the presence of a few suitcases.

During the changeover day(s) (some buildings split the changeover day by floors), departing owners are normally requested to leave about 10am and new owners to enter from about 4pm onwards. During the interim period, the apartments are cleaned and made ready for the new owner.

Now you might well ask where the catch is. When structured properly, there is none. After all, a timeshare building after completion of the selling is equivalent to a self-catering hotel with guaranteed occupancy and no recurring promotional costs, even if the developer has incurred higher initial marketing costs (selling fifty apartments to fifty families would be less costly than selling to 1,670 families). He has also eliminated the organisational costs which he would incur if he was to use the building for a normal resort rental programme. The net effect is that he can pass part of these savings on to the timeshare owner, who has also increased his initial costs but who will also in years to come make savings.

Words of Warning

The timeshare product, like any other consumer product recently introduced to the market, will attract all shades of entrepreneurs. As the industry matures, the undercapitalised entrepreneur will fall by the wayside leaving the industry to a combination of entrepreneurs who established themselves during the early days and the mainstream corporations who tend to enter the market place once the risks can be properly assessed.

The industry is currently in a period of rapid growth and it is important that you protect your interests when considering the purchase of a timeshare.

There have been and will surely continue to be a number of press items dramatising the excesses within the industry. Most of the articles tend to concentrate on practices in the lead-generation and sales systems. While the press will often sensationalise the situation, they are quite correct in pointing out that in certain areas of the Mediterranean, particularly in the Portuguese Algarve and Spain's Costa del Sol, timeshare touting has in certain places temporarily got out of hand.

The problem stems from the fact, as we will discuss in greater detail in Chapter 3, that the majority of us purchase timeshare on an emotional whim rather than from a cool and calculated viewpoint. Most timeshare schemes hire young people in their late teens and twenties to tout the product on the street and in bars and restaurants. These youngsters will endeavour to entice you to their resort with a promised gift, excursion, meal and so on. They are paid for the number of people they deliver to the resort and not usually for those who purchase. As such, they will endeavour to encourage as many people as possible to look at the resort.

This is fine until other resorts open up in the same area. It is then that the youngsters find themselves in a competitive battle for the attention of prospective buyers. The rapid growth of the industry has created severe tourist harassment in some areas. In 1986 the Portuguese Algarve authorities, in conjunction with the newly formed Portuguese Timeshare Association, limited street approaches to a maximum of five people in total employed per resort and now requires them to be both licensed and to wear an identifiable badge. This had a dramatic effect on the local industry and some 400 plus youngsters were suddenly out of employment. At the same time, it brought back a sense of sanity to the tourists when they ventured out of their holiday accommodation.

Another problem lies with some of the on-site sales consultants. While the vast majority of consultants are well trained and present their product and themselves in a proper manner, there is also the so called 'heat merchant' who will either misrepresent the product or attempt to browbeat the prospect into purchasing when in fact he or she does not really want the product.

There is a fine line between acceptable and unacceptable sales practices. It is the sales manager's job to secure the maximum number of sales at the minimum cost, but it is also his job to see that his staff present the product to you in the proper manner. One sales manager said to me that he continually reminds his staff that they must earn the right to make a sale. Until every objection has been satisfactorily answered, he has no right to ask for their cheque.

We have discussed above the two problems you may encounter at the outset when considering the purchase of a timeshare, particularly when you are on holiday. If you do not intend to purchase, the solution in both cases is simple. You must learn to say *no*!

There is another pitfall which is much more dangerous and can ultimately cause you financial distress. This deals with the product itself. If the resort is not properly structured, you can wind up with your right to a timeshare week being subordinate to a prior claim, for example the developer's mortgage on the property.

As we will discuss later on, the legal framework of timeshare schemes fall into two general categories. One is freehold ownership, and the other is rights of use for a fixed number of years sometimes with residual equity rights at the end. Due to the substantial initial preparation and marketing costs of the project, a number of developers will use their timeshare apartments as collateral for funding purposes. This is not necessarily a bad thing provided safeguards are built in to protect your investment against a sudden stoppage in sales or the financial reversal of the developer.

The most frequently used system is for the developer to allocate a portion of each sales price to the financial institution who, against this payment, releases his charge over your particular week. In the case of large firms such as Barratts, Wimpey, European Ferries or Marriott, the credibility of the firm alone is possibly sufficient to assure you that there will be no future ownership difficulties.

A number of resorts have taken steps to place the unencumbered ownership of the apartments with a third party who in turn will convey the rights directly to you. In this case, you have full assurance that your investment is secure. A number of resorts use trust companies or law firms for these purposes.

Many timeshare purchasers worry about the continued management of the resort once the selling cycle is complete. Generally speaking, there is little cause for worry once, as in the vast majority of instances, the timeshare owners control the management company through their home owners' association. The problem does arise in those cases where there is an interruption in the sales programme, leaving a number of unsold weeks in an apartment. In this event the developer may be 'taken over' by his bank or another party, either of whom may decide to discontinue timesharing. You may then find yourself owning a timeshare week in an apartment that is also being rented out. In those cases where rentals represent a substantial portion of the weeks throughout the year, there is a strong possibility that the quality and standards of the apartment will be down-graded to accommodate the rental market.

Another problem in the above instance is that the affiliation to the timeshare exchange (see Chapter 5) may be cancelled leaving you with no opportunity to exchange your timeshare for other locations.

It is fair to say that few timeshare projects encounter any major problem that can not be resolved by a refunding programme. From a practical sense, once timeshare weeks have been legally conveyed in one or more apartments at a resort, it is difficult if not impossible to change the direction of the project. Your assurance lies in the simple truth that the greater the number of weeks sold, the greater your assurance the project will continue as a timeshare scheme. We have provided in the latter part of this chapter a checklist for your use before purchasing your timeshare. (See also the checklist 'Your Place in the Sun', issued by the Department of Trade and Industry, reproduced as an Appendix on pages 118–19).

Advantages and Disadvantages

Whatever the basis of your decision, first and foremost your timeshare purchase is a long-term commitment that allows you to buy future holidays at today's prices. So, for example, whether you enjoy spending Christmas in the sunshine of the Canary Islands and the Caribbean, or prefer the cooler months of the Algarve or the Costa del Sol to sample the vast range of golf courses, or simply want to stay at home and enjoy the delights of rural England and the more rugged areas of Scotland and Wales, holiday timesharing gives you the opportunity to buy a share in a holiday home at your favourite resort at the time of year when you prefer to take a break.

TABLE 3
GROWTH IN HOTEL PRICES DURING THE LAST FIFTEEN YEARS

Year	Pounds Sterling	Percent Increase over 1970
1970	4.27	—
1975	7.00	63
1980	24.00	462
1985	43.20	901
1986 (est.)	48.20	1,029

Prices are at AA appointed four-star hotels in the provinces of England and Wales. They cover bed and breakfast per night, including a ten per cent service charge, plus VAT at eight per cent up to 1979 and fifteen per cent from 1980.

Although you own your unit and week 'time', one thing you do not need to worry about is the possibility of becoming bored by having to return to the same resort year after year at the same time. Holiday timesharing only really came into its own in the mid-1970s with the introduction of the exchange system. At present there are two major international organisations – Interval

International (II) and Resort Condominiums International (RCI) – providing an exchange facility, and any worthwhile resort considers it essential to enter one or other system in order to be able to offer that added attraction to its owners. This means you can swap your time and place whenever you feel the need for a change of scenery for another resort in another location in any of the countries in which your project's system has members.

When you buy your holiday timeshare you are guaranteed occupancy rights for a given number of years, so there are no reservation problems. This is one of the major benefits of a ready made holiday – all you need do is to get there.

Provided you have done your homework, the savings start the minute you sign the purchase agreement and complete the financial transaction. The cost of the unit is a once-only expense, but there is an annual maintenance fee applicable per week owned. Someone has to look after your holiday home in your absence, although the amount of money involved is comparatively small (see Chapter 4).

You may have placed your money in the timeshare property instead of placing it on deposit or investing it. The future value of your timeshare should, after three to five years, equal or surpass the interest you might have earned from another investment.

There are also ways to make savings. For example, in a two-bedroom unit which sleeps six there is usually a sofa bed in the sitting room, so you can invite an extra couple of friends along or have guests to spend the night. Again, because you know when you are going away you can budget well in advance and get good deals on air fares, car hire and so on. You will probably not even have to look further than your resort management, who are usually in the best position to offer you the most favourable terms through their contacts. It could be said that it is in their best interests to provide you with whatever leads to a happy and trouble-free holiday for, unlike the one-time renter, you are an owner who will return year after year.

Timesharing is all about luxury. There is really little reason to tie up substantial amounts of money if you can just as easily rent the same accommodation elsewhere. Timesharing is about giving you a higher standard of holiday accommodation and lifestyle.

In the majority of resorts the units are self-catering, although there are usually on-site restaurants, bars and snack-bars. You may not like the idea of cooking when on holiday, but the majority of timeshare kitchens are modern with labour-saving devices.

Throughout you will find that timeshare units are usually furnished and equipped to far higher standards than at home. Although standards vary by country and region, comfort and ease are the norm, with tasteful colour schemes. You do not have to worry about bringing along bulky packages of linen and utensils – everything should be there, from the sheets to the nailbrush to the tiniest mustard spoon. In most cases there will be plenty of comfortable seating, ample table-top space, family games and a radio-cassette player; if there is no television, then at least there will be a socket so that you can take advantage of the rental facility provided by the management. (Some resorts in very hot climates, and very often ski resorts, know from experience that their owners are hardly ever at home except to sleep – and it makes a small saving in the total budget.) The bathrooms are usually well equipped and well lit, with bidets and showers (often with special high-pressure jets), and some have baths with impulse jets or whirlpools; there are even units with built-in saunas.

Outside the unit are the on-site facilities and amenities. Most resorts have at least one restaurant and/or snack bar and a bar/lounge area, a swimming pool, either indoors or outdoors, and a children's play area. Tennis courts are popular, so are squash courts and fully equipped gymnasium. Variations on the theme depend on climate, country, and the image being presented. These can include professional golf courses, hunting and shooting, scuba diving and deep-sea fishing, private marinas, skiing, and a whole host of other pastimes.

More often than not the immediate facilities can be enjoyed free of charge as the installation/upkeep costs have been allowed for in the purchase price and a percentage of the annual weekly maintenance fee. You may have to pay though for specialised sports; you should be made fully aware of this through the brochures and sales information before you make your decision to buy.

With your holiday timeshare there should be no hidden charges. Everything should be stated in the documents – but if not, you should at least be able to have sight of any relevant papers.

Before you buy, do make sure the resort is 'you'. Do not go for a jazzy Costa del Sol sunspot when you would far rather spend most of your time hiking in the Scottish Highlands – even though you can swap. It is better to buy into a resort in Scotland and swap to the sun. Notwithstanding the allure of the glossy brochures, *do remember it is far better to buy into a resort which comes closest to your favourite holiday haunt.* You can always swap to other extremes in the odd years when the mood dictates. Still on this note, take a good look at the design and décor and make sure you can live with them – they cannot be changed to suit your taste. Also, check the amenities; if you feel there are grandiose schemes that will not be justified by full use, take heed – they could land everyone with higher than normal maintenance costs.

Of comfort is the fact that in the short history of holiday timesharing the adage is once a timeshare resort always a timeshare resort. There may be a temporary fading from the big scene, but this is more often due to a change in ownership and/or management. Afterwards it is a case of all stops out to catch up. This being said, it is absolutely vital that you make sure your title to (right to use) your resort is secure – and then you are safe. There are several insurance companies offering timeshare-title insurance schemes.

There are many factors which can be of concern. One is the long term competence and stability of your resort's on-site management. Another is the competence of the exchange companies. Here you will be bound by whichever system is being used by your resort. However, the rules of the companies usually are quite simple, and providing you follow them as closely as you can, there should be few, if any, problems. Yet a third factor which can raise a discordant note concerns the ease by which you can resell your time, for whatever reason. There are no guaranteed to be workable or tried-and-tested paths anywhere in the world as yet; this secondary market is only just emerging. There is a handful of companies operating in this market in the United States at present. In Europe the monopoly lies in Great Britain with, perhaps, only a couple of recognised outlets.

In all these matters you, as a prospective buyer, should expect to have clear answers to certain questions.

Let us review the potential pitfalls and establish a mini checklist of items to verify before we buy:

Mini Timeshare Checklist

A. Before you purchase
Learn to say 'no' until you are completely satisfied and prepared to make a decision.

B. When you purchase
1. Are you acquiring unencumbered rights to occupation?
If no, is your money partially or wholly held on deposit (with a third party) until your rights are conveyed to you?
If no, is the company of sufficient size to assure you of its credibility?
2. Do the timeshare owners have a majority vote over the home owners' association and control the management company?
If no, what safeguards are there to assure you of continued high standards of furnishings and maintenance?
What protection do you have against excessive increases in the annual maintenance fee?
3. Is the maintenance fee based on cost plus a fixed percentage fee to the management?
If no, who pays the difference if the expenses are greater than the income (ie index-linked schemes).
4. Is the resort affiliated to a major exchange organisation such as II or RCI?
If no, why not? If in doubt, ask to telephone II or RCI from the resort to verify affiliation status.
5. Is the resort a member of the British Property Timeshare Association (or another reputable trade association), or if overseas, a member of their national timeshare assocation?
If no, why not?

C. Credibility Checklist
1. Are there ten or more apartments for sale in the timesharing format? (If less, project may be economically unviable.)
2. How many weeks in how many apartments have been sold to date? (The greater the number of weeks sold the greater the future timesharing commitment.)
3. Does the resort use a third party to receive payments and convey legal documents? (It is not necessary, but often provides greater protection to purchaser.)

4. Who is the developer? Is it an established company?

If you are completely satisfied with the information provided to you, you may well proceed to purchase on the spot, as in many cases you will receive a 'first day decision' benefit in the form of price discount or gift.

If you are partially satisfied, you may wish to leave a nominal deposit (which may not be refundable) to hold your desired week(s) until you verify any outstanding questions.

If you are not satisfied, do not be intimidated, say *no*!

If the legal documents are confusing or unclear but at the same time you wish to purchase, one solution is to request that your solicitor contacts the developer's solicitor by telephone in order to clarify the situation. Unless your solicitor understands timesharing documentation, it may prove to be a costly exercise for him to review them in detail, whereas a quick solicitor-to-solicitor telephone call could resolve the question.

The checklist above is contained in Chapter 6, where five rules that should be followed before you purchase your timeshare are suggested.

Once the points above and in Chapter 6 have been clarified satisfactorily, everything else should fall into place. There should then be no fears that your resort will depreciate over the years through lack of care. Nor should you have to worry about the management producing an outrageous annual budget causing your share of the maintenance fees to rocket out of all proportion. Holiday timesharing has been operating in one way or another since the early 1960s and it is to be hoped most of the earlier hiccups have now been eliminated.

Having touched on the advantages and disadvantages of holiday timesharing, it is only in an ideal world that everything is perfect. When you are making a purchase involving a large financial outlay, for example a car, you do your homework before making the final commitment. It is not that difficult because as soon as the idea starts to germinate in your mind you immediately put a price-tag on the item. The size and capacity of the car is determined by occupancy, frequency of use, mileage and so on; the make is determined by how a model will perform according to your expectations. Exactly the same parameters apply to buying a holiday timeshare; you know more or less what you want and it is just a case of making sure you buy that which is most suitable for your needs for the foreseeable future.

Timesharing around the World

English language variations: time-sharing, multi-ownership, time ownership, holiday ownership, property timesharing, vacation sharing, holiday vacations.

FRANCE: temps partagé multipropriété
SPAIN: multipropriedad
MEXICO: tiempo compartido
PORTUGAL: habitacao periodica
GERMANY: teilzeiteigentum
ITALY: multiproprieta

The proof of the pudding is to know just what timeshare owners think about their purchases. Professor Ragatz has done an analysis of timeshare owners and his results show a remarkably high satisfaction rate throughout the world.*

TABLE 4
REACTIONS OF TIMESHARE OWNERS

	UK	Canada	USA	Australia
	Per cent of respondents			
A. General Satisfaction				
Very satisfied	50.2	41.6	32.7	54.0
Satisfied	39.6	46.5	45.8	36.9
So-so	8.6	9.2	15.9	7.1
Dissatisfied	1.6	1.7	3.4	1.6
Very dissatisfied	—	1.0	2.2	0.4
Total	100.0	100.0	100.0	100.0
B. Would Purchase with Hindsight				
Yes	84.7	73.6	62.5	79.5
No	5.2	10.0	19.0	9.2
Don't know	10.0	16.4	18.5	11.4
Total	100.0	100.0	100.0	100.0

*The Ragatz Organisation is probably the foremost research organisation within the world timeshare industry. It has been commissioned to undertake numerous studies for the US domestic market and throughout the world. At the time of going to press the Ragatz Organisation is preparing an updated study on the British timeshare owner.

Perhaps the most important point made in Table 4 is that with hindsight more than seventy-five per cent of all timeshare buyers agree they would still purchase their timeshare. And it appears that a substantial number of buyers, upon reflection, will purchase additional weeks either at their own resort or at another resort. It is now possible to purchase at two or more timeshare schemes, combine the weeks and exchange to a third resort for the sum total. Thus, many timeshare owners across the world are buying at both summer and winter resorts and using them to take extended holidays from time to time in more distant places.

TABLE 5
WORLD TIMESHARE GROWTH BETWEEN 1985 AND 1986

| | 1985 | | 1986 (est.) | |
	Owners (000)	Resorts	Owners (000)	Resorts
Europe	230	260	295	290
UK (inc. in Europe total)	(50)	(43)	(85)	(55)
North America	750	1,050	1,100	850
Mexico	60	100	95	115
Central/S. America	17	28	22	34
Caribbean	20	48	23	54
Africa	28	36	35	38
Asia	250	290	274	330
Japan (inc. in Asia total)	(230)	(275)	(250)	(300)
Australasia	16	40	20	42
1985 total of new owners/resorts	1588	1998		

It is evident from these figures that the industry is flourishing, with an increasing number of timeshare schemes and buyers, and with worldwide distribution.

1 Holiday Timeshare Schemes Explained

As already defined in the Introduction, by buying a holiday timeshare you acquire the right to use a holiday-home unit for one or more days or weeks each year for a successive number of years. How these periods of time are apportioned is another matter.

The basis is the annual calendar which, apart from its natural fifty-two weekly divisions, is often further divided into three seasons, high, middle and low, which are then usually colour coded. II and RCI issue calendars to their affiliated member resorts, which are still fairly widely used. However, as seasonal classifications vary according to country, climate and holiday patterns and flights to certain areas are only obtainable on weekdays as opposed to the more traditional Saturdays, and because of the efforts being made to provide for more flexible schemes of ownership, it is now no longer feasible to impose a standard regime.

It is not as complicated as it sounds on first hearing. Apart from Christmas, New Year, Easter and school holidays, summer dictates high season in a hot climate and winter dictates high season at ski resorts. Again, at present the only British international direct flight in and out of the island of Lanzarote is on a Thursday, so it would be illogical to try and adhere to the traditional Saturday changeover. As for flexibility – it is nice to know that your Easter week actually 'floats' to coincide with the annual change in dates.

Fixed and Floating Time

Fixed Time
The most commonly accepted form of holiday timesharing is by periods of weeks or multiples thereof, where the days and dates of entry and departure are fixed in the annual resort calendar for the entire length of your term of ownership. If a resort is very large, it may spread its check-in check-out system over two days, and you

will be allocated whichever day is more convenient, bearing in mind that flights may not always be direct. The one constant, however, is usually the timing – check in after 4pm and check out by 10am, giving the management a full half day in which to prepare your home for your arrival.

Floating Time

Floating time, as the phrase implies, is a system which allows for greater flexibility within given periods, usually in the middle and low seasons. When you buy floating time you still buy as many weeks as you want, but you also acquire the option to reserve these weeks each year, at a time you choose, within the appropriate prearranged limits. If you do not make a reservation, then your resort management will designate the dates and notify you accordingly. The check-in check-out systems operate as for fixed time.

Fixed and Floating Time

Although a combination of fixed and floating time has been in use in Europe for a number of years, largely to help overcome the problems connected with Easter Sunday moving back and forth over a period of some six weeks, it has only been introduced comparatively recently over a wider season and in other areas around the world.

Generally speaking, Easter (whatever the date), Christmas to New Year and the peak holiday periods have fixed owners. These times of the year are very much in demand, so it is only natural that they do not carry the same flexibility otherwise there would be a mad scramble and too many disappointments.

The middle and low seasons, which are less popular for main holidays, are then allowed to float into the system, giving those who want more flexibility the option to use their resort for the number of weeks they have bought at any time they wish during whichever season by making an advance reservation each year.

In all this there do exist people who prefer to go on holiday during the off-peak seasons and, furthermore, at the same time each year. Provision is usually made for such instances; you are then able to 'fix' your chosen week or weeks by paying a nominal premium in addition to the purchase price, and this secures your preference for the duration of the lease.

Fixed and Floating Units

Fixed Units

In most cases, when you purchase a specific week (fixed time) you also purchase a specific apartment/villa/unit. You then know when you are going on holiday and can visualise your unit's interior and its situation at the resort. These details will put your mind at ease, particularly if you are disabled or the sort of person who dislikes heights, when the possibility of being put on the fifteenth floor of a building would not be appealing.

Resorts which have been developed from refurbishing existing structures, such as stately homes, have very few identical units. Each unit has its own personality. Some may have spiral staircases and others, space permitting, may have bathrooms adjoining each bedroom.

Floating Units

There are now an increasing number of resorts offering floating units. As mentioned already, fixed weeks are usually associated with fixed units, likewise floating weeks are usually associated with floating units.

It really is a question of offering you the greatest flexibility possible. By floating both weeks and units, the resort operates just like a hotel. It offers you the widest choice of both time and accommodation.

If you enjoy spontaneous holidays or varying the dates each year, then floating weeks and units are for you. The same thing applies if you are obliged to take your holiday at the same time each year.

In cases where these weeks or units which are floating are limited, make sure that others' demands are spread throughout the year, otherwise you will have difficulty obtaining what you want.

Resorts offering floating time and units often operate on a priority system. In general, when the manager receives two booking requests posted on the same day for a specific time (or unit) slot, he will allocate it to the owner who perhaps was unable to obtain his first choice the previous year.

You will normally find that many of the regional resorts are using floating time/units for their low periods, as they find that while many continue to use the resort for their primary holiday many also enjoy using it out of season for that spontaneous second holiday.

Split Weeks

Recently many resorts are beginning to use split weeks. Perhaps you wish to spend a few days in London sightseeing, shopping and going to the theatre. Afterwards a few days in the countryside, where it is more relaxing and quieter, may be appealing to you.

More and more regional and urban resorts are opening their doors to the split-week idea. At these resorts, in addition to owning your week(s) you have the opportunity to split them into two, three or in some cases seven parts.

Generally speaking, you are permitted to split the week into two parts, for example Thursday to Saturday and Sunday to Wednesday, but resorts vary. Should you use the weekend section first then you would be obliged to take the weekday section on your next visit.

In some cases, you are permitted to draw down one day at a time. You will find that these resorts tend to be more hotel orientated and located in urban centres. But there are certain limitations as it could really confuse things if everyone opted for weekends and not weekdays. Generally split weeks are used for off-season periods or permitted only when all owners have had the opportunity to request their week(s).

Fractional Interests

While most people purchase timeshares by the week, and rarely for more than three to four weeks, another market is developing for families who have extended holiday time, are retired or seek rental income opportunities.

You may buy timeshares by the month, by six-week periods or even by a quarter of a year! These are called fractional interests. They are identical to a normal timeshare purchase except for the extended length of time and the manner in which you are allocated your occupancy periods each year.

Many resorts offering fractional interests structure the occupancy periods on a rotation basis. For example, in one year you may use if for the first two weeks of January, the first two weeks of July, the month of January or for the first quarter of the year. In year two, you are moved forward a notch. Thus, you would have the second two weeks of January and July, February or the second quarter of the year.

As the rotation continues you move forward until you have passed through the entire year.

Rotation Schedule.

As a purchaser you will join a rotation scheme which is laid out below. For example, if you chose weeks 28 & 29 as your prime summer allocation in the first year (C) you would also be allocated weeks 14 & 44 to make up your 4 weeks period.

The following year you would move on to weeks 16 & 17 and weeks 51 & 4 (D). The rotation would then continue yearly as shown in the diagram.

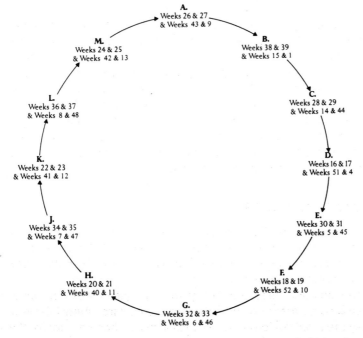

A.
Weeks 26 & 27
& Weeks 43 & 9

B.
Weeks 38 & 39
& Weeks 15 & 1

M.
Weeks 24 & 25
& Weeks 42 & 13

C.
Weeks 28 & 29
& Weeks 14 & 44

L.
Weeks 36 & 37
& Weeks 8 & 48

D.
Weeks 16 & 17
& Weeks 51 & 4

K.
Weeks 22 & 23
& Weeks 41 & 12

E.
Weeks 30 & 31
& Weeks 5 & 45

J.
Weeks 34 & 35
& Weeks 7 & 47

F.
Weeks 18 & 19
& Weeks 52 & 10

H.
Weeks 20 & 21
& Weeks 40 & 11

G.
Weeks 32 & 33
& Weeks 6 & 46

PLEASE NOTE: Weeks 2, 3, 49 & 50 have been taken out of the rotation schedule in order to carry out necessary maintenance to your villa.

Fig 1 Rotation schedule of Marbellamar, Marbella–CoOwnership Ltd

Resorts which have peak periods, such as ski resorts, will usually offer fixed fractional interests which do not rotate through the year.

You will find that floating time and units are less used in fractional interests than in traditional one-week multiple timeshares.

Fractional interests will appeal to many who have extended holiday time. As a rule of thumb, the longer the interval purchased, the more advantageous the purchase price, as it means the developer is selling to fewer people and cutting down his costs, the savings of which he can pass on to you.

The recent introduction of floating time/units, split weeks and fractional interests has brought a new dimension to the market, giving much greater flexibility as to when and for how long you can use your holiday home.

Ownership Formulas

While holiday timesharing is essentially pre-purchasing future holidays, the method of purchasing these holiday rights is similar to the purchase of rights to occupy property. Many of us who are settled own our own homes. If we are urban dwellers, we may have a long or a short lease or rent for a fixed period of time.

Depending upon the resort and country you will normally purchase either 'ownership', as with a private dwelling, or the 'right to occupy', similar to a lease or rental agreement.

When you purchase your timeshare on an ownership basis, you receive a beneficial interest in your particular unit and common parts of the whole property for the time you purchase. When you purchase the right to occupy you receive an agreement that merely secures your right to occupy for that period of time each year.

There are many variations to ownership and rights to occupy. The subject is too detailed to cover in its entirety in this publication. Summarised below are the most common systems but it is suggested you contact a legal expert for more detailed information and advice.

Divided Freehold

Timeshares sold under this formula convey to you a title deed with the same rights and privileges that you would receive when you purchase a home. Your title deed is registered as evidence of your ownership. In Spain and Portugal the deed is known as an Escritura.

Companies

In France and some other countries, timeshares are usually sold on a share-subscription basis. This means that you acquire your ownership interest when you purchase shares in a company that holds title to the property. The shares either carry a covenant or are broken down into classifications that delegate to the shareholder the right to occupy a certain period of time in a certain unit each year. Once again, you will find variations, for example between fixed and floating weeks/units. Or you may find that the more shares you buy the greater your choice of when you can take your holiday and the unit size.

Swiss-based Hapimag, Europe's first timeshare-orientated group, now has over 40,000 shareholders who have rights – depending upon their number of shares – to draw down on close to 2,000 apartments in resorts in eleven European countries.

Founded by Dr Hans Schalch in 1963, the Baar-based group pioneered the concept of floating time and floating units by purchasing over the years a wide collection of resorts on behalf of its owners. Hapimag and France's Clubhotel timeshare group, part of Club Méditerranée, vie for first place as the largest timeshare organisation in Europe.

Leases

This is identical to taking a lease on an apartment or house for a fixed number of years. It only varies from a normal lease in that you are limited to a certain occupancy time(s) each year. Most timeshare leases run for a minimum of twenty-five to thirty years. A few leases extend beyond this time-frame, for example when a developer prefers to offer ownership in perpetuity but the law of the land does not provide a legal basis for it.

Conversely, with boats, where their useful lifespan is limited, you will find short leases of five to ten years.

Licences

The right to occupy under a licence is similar to a lease, but it does not convey the same degree of rights. You will often find a licence offered in cases where a lease may require a greater degree of documentation, filing and negotiations with government authorities. The Greek and Maltese governments restrict the number of years for a non-national to own a lease on property in their countries. In many parts of the United States, the sale of leases in excess of a certain number of years requires extensive documentation and filing with the regulatory bodies, whereas a licence does not.

Club Membership

This type of occupancy right is very popular in the United Kingdom and elsewhere where the prevailing law, for example, does not allow for timeshare-ownership systems. It is also popular in many Mediterranean countries where the units, and indeed sometimes the entire resort, is sold to a foreign company which then sells rights to occupy.

Most club membership schemes use a system whereby the property title is vested with a reputable third party such as a bank, trustee, law or accountancy firm. The third party binds himself to keep the property free and clear from all mortgages or charges for the life of the agreement, usually twenty-five to thirty years. This party then passes the rights to occupy for this period of time to a club set up for this purpose. The club has its own constitution that binds all the club members together. This covers such items as entry and departure dates, maintenance charges and so on.

You then acquire a membership into the club. The club certificate entitles you to occupy either a fixed or floating time in a unit(s). The club scheme is very popular as it reduces the legal documentation needed for ownership schemes and provides an effective and easily understood method for the purchaser.

It is important to note that, before you purchase into a club membership scheme, you should make sure that the title of the property has been conveyed to the third party. In cases where it has not yet taken place (property conveyances in some countries can take months), you should have the opportunity to block your funds until the property has been conveyed. Should you have any doubts about the legal documentation, you would be advised to contact your solicitor and ask him to consult with the law firm that

Allen House, Kensington, London, England – an urban resort

prepared the documents. (Fig 2 shows a typical British timeshare legal document.)

Timeshare legal documentation can be complicated and is often confusing not only to the prospective purchaser but also to the solicitor. Many timeshare schemes, based outside Britain and marketed essentially to non-nationals, eg those in Spain and Portugal, use offshore trusts based in the Channel Islands or the Isle of Man to hold the asset and pass on rights of occupancy.

The offshore base is a convenient way to hold in trust the title to the apartments and to create a legally constituted club whose shares are then sold to the timeshare purchasers. These shares carry the right to occupy the timeshare apartments. The net effect is that developer and purchaser taxes are minimised, title is held in a stable tax environment, documents are in English and the laws covering club membership, trusts and longterm leases/licences can be used.

While the 'offshore vehicle' is convenient it creates for the uninitiated rather cumbersome and confusing documentation which can often lead to certain doubts on the purchaser side.

As a rule, offshore trust/club membership schemes are well structured and copies of all the agreements are available at time of purchase. It is usually also possible to obtain on the spot copies of all the documents. These include:

Trustee deed: governs the relationship of the trust commitment with developer and the club

Club constitution: governs the timeshare owner's rules and regulations for the use of the timeshare units and the voting rights thereof

Management agreement: governs the procedures and costs associated with managing the apartments and the common areas

Management certificate and form of surrender: conveys the rights of occupancy and the right to assign, sell or bequeath these rights to a third party.

In all instances, your first protection is the credibility of the

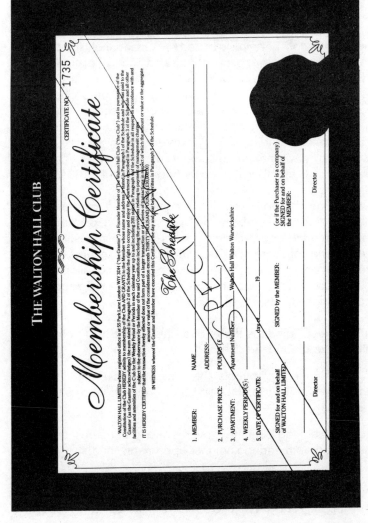

THE WALTON HALL CLUB

Membership Certificate

CERTIFICATE NO. 1735

WALTON HALL LIMITED whose registered office is at 55 Park Lane London W1Y 3DH ("the Grantor") as Founder Member of The Walton Hall Club ("the Club") and in pursuance of the Constitution of the Club HEREBY admits to membership of the Club AND GRANTS to the Member whose name and address are stated in Paragraph 1 of the Schedule and who has paid to the Grantor (as the Grantor acknowledges) the sum stated in Paragraph 2 of the Schedule the right to occupy and enjoy the Apartment described in Paragraph 3 of the Schedule and all other facilities and amenities of the Club for the Weekly Period or Periods in each calendar year up to and including 2011 stated in Paragraph 4 of the Schedule in all respects in accordance with and subject to the observance by the Member of the said Constitution including the provisions relating to the payment of management charges

IT IS HEREBY CERTIFIED that the transaction hereby effected does not form part of a larger transaction or of a series of transactions in respect of which the amount or value or the aggregate amount or value of the consideration exceeds THIRTY THOUSAND POUNDS (£30,000,00)

IN WITNESS whereof the Grantor and Member have executed this Certificate the day and year below written in Paragraph 5 of the Schedule

The Schedule

1. MEMBER: NAME: _____

                    ADDRESS: _____

2. PURCHASE PRICE: POUNDS (£ _____

3. APARTMENT: Apartment Number _____ Walton Hall Walton Warwickshire

4. WEEKLY PERIOD(S): _____

5. DATE OF CERTIFICATE: _____ day of _____ 19___

SIGNED for and on behalf   SIGNED by the MEMBER: (or if the Purchaser is a company)
of WALTON HALL LIMITED   SIGNED for and on behalf of
                                                                 the MEMBER:

_____   _____   _____
Director   Director

Fig 2 Typical British timeshare legal document

developer. If you have reservations at this level, the next layer of protection is the companies that are associated with the scheme. Are the legal, accounting, trustee and other professional parties well known and respected? Should your doubts persist, it is well worth having your solicitor contact the developer's solicitor to review the legal structure.

2 Choosing Your Resort

Having ascertained what holiday timesharing is and how it works and having learned something about the legal aspects of its operation, the next step is really the most important one in the whole process.

Although the following chapter deals with making your purchase, anyone who reads this guide will probably already have made the financial commitment, even if only in their minds. Hopefully, this chapter will steer the reader through the myriad permutations of resorts, locations and amenities and lead them towards the best possible holiday timeshare for their particular holiday needs and available capital.

Before launching into any details it is well to remember the international battle cry of successful holiday timeshare promoters: 'Location! Location! Location!' Perhaps, by the end of this chapter, but definitely by the end of this book, you will also agree that this should apply to timeshare purchasers.

Types of Resorts

There are three different types of resorts in which holiday timeshare projects may be found. These are called: urban resorts, regional resorts and destination resorts. Urban resorts, as the name implies, are resorts in big cities like London, Paris, New York, San Francisco and so on. They are usually found incorporated into classic, serviced, apartment blocks, because the essential amenities for looking after such a scheme are already in place. Another variation is the conversion of a floor or floors of a hotel – again for the same reasons. There are one or two examples in Great Britain of how the hotel conversion can be done successfully but, because of their location, they do not qualify under this heading.

The object of an urban resort is essentially to attract two types of buyers. It is firstly for those in the business community who use a centre with great frequency and for whom it is far more conducive to their business activities to own such an apartment rather than frequent a continual string of impersonal hotels. Secondly it is for holidaymakers who love the arts, the bright lights and all the other attractions of a big city.

Regional resorts are those situated in areas which are easily accessible within a few hours of your home, either by road or by rail.

By virtue of its size and geographical location, Great Britain has mainly regional and urban resorts. At the opposite end of the scale is the United States; whilst the country is in itself vast, there are, for example, holiday timeshares in the Pocono Mountains which come under the heading of regional resorts, being a gentle drive from New York. The other point about regional resorts is that they are usually associated with second holidays.

The general pattern is for people to choose a location which involves a considerable amount of travel and effort to arrive for their main holiday during the year. Then, if they want an off-peak break, they probably choose somewhere which only involves hopping into the car or on to a train for an hour or so.

Destination resorts, by far the most numerous anywhere the world over, are those which are recognised as being the most popular holiday areas in a country. Generally speaking they are reached by air or sea, but in any event there is usually a considerable distance to be travelled.

Among these are the big ski resorts in central Europe; the shores of the Mediterranean and Portugal and the Canary Islands; Florida and California in the United States; Surfer's Paradise on Australia's Queensland coastline; even Cornwall on the southwest tip of England.

Destination resorts are also considered to be places people frequent for their major holiday each year.

Country	Destination Resort	Urban Resort	Regional Resort
Great Britain	Cornwall	London	The Trossachs
France	The Riviera	Paris	The Dordogne
Spain	Costa del Sol	Madrid	Sierra Nevada
Portugal	Algarve	Lisbon	Cascais
United States	Florida	New York	The Poconos
India	Goa	New Delhi	Kodakainal
Australia	Surfer's Paradise	—	Kyneton

Of course there are no hard and fast rules as to where anyone should or should not go on holiday. The chief purpose of this exercise is to provide a timeshare industry classification to help you, the buyer. With over 1,750 holiday timeshare resorts, as already mentioned, it would seem to be necessary. The table on page 39 shows how the system of classification works, though these are only examples – there is more to Spain than just the Costa del Sol, for instance. But at least it will give you some idea of how to start looking and where.

It is virtually impossible to try and explain , other than briefly, the types of resorts available everywhere around the world – that would need a publication all on its own. For the purpose of this guide we will continue to concentrate throughout on Europe, with special emphasis on Great Britain.

Holiday timesharing in Europe stretches as far east as Turkey, south to the Canary Islands, and north to Scandinavia.

Types of Projects

A holiday timeshare development is usually a building or series of buildings having a number of apartments, lodges or villas containing a range of units varying in size from a studio to three or four bedrooms on the grand scale, at least one full bathroom or shower room, and an open-plan kitchen and living room with a settee that converts into a double bed. In the larger units the master bedroom usually has its own en suite bathroom. The quality of the fixtures and fittings, particularly in Britain, is very high. Some units even have a built-in sauna and/or jacuzzi, perhaps a barbecue area and also, but less frequently, a private swimming pool.

The buildings can be stately home conversions – which are mostly found in Britain. They can be hotel conversions. They can be a series of purpose-built villas which form their own mini-village. Most have on-site bars and restaurants, and a variety of recreational facilities that depend, to a large extent, on where the projects are located and what 'image' they are trying to present to entice you across their thresholds.

It took a while for holiday timesharing to catch on in Great Britain, but since about 1982 there has been a rapid growth in the number of resorts available. Certain far-sighted and astute developers bought up stately homes or well established hotels – all of which were either white elephants or financial liabilities as they stood. With a touch of ingenuity they renovated and refurbished them and turned them into top-quality holiday timeshare resorts, each one being totally outstanding in its own right because of its historical background.

The use of stately homes – in Great Britain in particular – is something in which Europe is ahead of most other continents. While everyone can compete equally with interiors and leisure facilities, they are often unable to do so from a historical standpoint. Britain possibly ranks highest in the world for its original thinking and great diversity of available resorts from which you can choose.

It can be safely assumed that Britain's stately home holiday timeshare schemes will shortly be emulated in Europe. The French have already started, albeit under the guidance of a British developer, and the Benelux countries, Austria, Germany, Switzerland and Italy are all sitting on superb mansions and castles that no longer in their present form have a viable economic role to play.

What to Expect at the Resort

The individual 'product', in professional terminology, varies by country or national characteristics, and of course by climate. These factors govern virtually the whole of a holiday timeshare resort operation from inception and through every other stage to the end of the lease.

You only need to look around you to understand the basic principles. Great Britain has a temperamental climate with no guaranteed summer, so your timeshare home will have to be warmly furnished, include a television set, and the kitchen will have plenty of facilities for cooking. The amenities will probably include an indoor, heated, swimming pool, saunas, squash courts, gymnasia and similar places where you can be sheltered from the elements. Of course you can choose a resort where there is tennis, horse riding, golf, windsurfing, sailing, hiking and so on, but unfortunately you cannot plan your holiday in advance based on the weather!

Insofar as northern and central Europe are concerned, with the exception of the ski resorts, the pattern is very similar because of the climate.

Ski resorts have their own rules and regulations. The timeshare apartments are usually self catering, but the emphasis is on utility and serviceability rather than the ultimate in luxury. It is traditional that skiers are out all day on the slopes and out most of the night on après-ski activities and meals seem to be consumed in restaurants and bars.

Resorts on the Iberian peninsula and in and around the Mediterranean show a different attitude to design, fixtures, fittings and facilities. There is more emphasis on balconies and patios, for example. Although some resorts do have fitted carpets, because of high temperatures most of the year, tiled floors are more likely because they are traditional, very cool and easy to keep clean, particularly where they are adjacent to beaches and there is a constant trail of sand.

In hot climates the emphasis is on lightness and airiness and lots of white paint. Spain often uses dark oak for the furnishings, so the colours balance each other. A few resorts only have rental facilities for television sets because they know their owners will be out most of the time. The kitchens, although well equipped, do not need the same extensive range of cooking facilities as their cold-climate counterparts – the French, Spanish, Italians, Greeks and Portuguese traditionally use grills most of the time and gas or electric hobs rather than ovens.

The facilities on site and nearby can include swimming pools, tennis courts, horse riding, golf, windsurfing, water skiing, sailing, fishing, scuba diving, and even deep-sea fishing. Although it depends on the exact package presented by a resort, as already mentioned you will usually find everything on site is included in the purchase price and the annual maintenance fee – which means there is nothing additional to pay – but you should be able to find what is included through the sales brochures before you commit yourself. Where any such facilities are available but not on site, you will usually find your resort management has been able to negotiate special rates to make things easier for you.

In all this there are several resorts which offer all-inclusive specialist activities, apart from winter sports. There are resorts with their own golf courses; those with salmon-fishing rights; others have hunting and shooting rights; water sports might be the theme; and coastal resorts in warmer climates may even offer deep-sea fishing.

How to Find out What is Available

In the early days it was a little difficult to know where to start looking for information. Now holiday timesharing has been granted its own section in the national and regional press, and every so often you will find special features, particularly in *The Daily Telegraph,* the *Daily Mail* and *The Times.* There are also two publications, *Homes Overseas* and *Homes and Travel Abroad,* both of which are obtainable from major newsagents. The exchange organisations, Interval International and Resort Condominiums International, each publish an annual directory of all the resorts around the world belonging to their respective systems, and you can buy copies by contacting the resort services departments at their London offices (see Useful Addresses section).

In addition, you will find exhibitions are held in various centres around the country at intervals. They tend to last two or three days, but invariably the last day is a Saturday, which gives the weekday working population a fair chance to attend.

There is now a trend towards brokerage/marketing firms with a wide variety of resorts on their books whose job it is to help you find what you want and, perhaps, save you a lot of foot-slogging. For this service they must obviously expect some form of financial gain — but generally speaking, it is a buyer's market and any commissions due are payable by the seller.

Another innovation is the try-buy scheme, mainly available through brokerage and marketing firms. The way it works is that they arrange for you to rent a week or two at a resort where you feel you would like to become an owner and, in the event that you decide to buy at that resort, the developer will deduct the rental price from the purchase price for each week bought. If, for some reason, you do not wish to commit yourself to that specific place, your only obligation equates with that of a normal, self-catering, rental holiday.

How to Decide

The whole purpose of this book is to steer you, the prospective timeshare purchaser, through, if you will, a minefield laid by the protagonists and antagonists.

The similarity between buying, say, a new car, and a timeshare has already been described; remember that you would hardly accept delivery of your chosen vehicle without first taking it for a test drive. The same goes for the latter.

Purchaser Checkpoints

1. Your holiday habits
What is your annual holiday entitlement?
What type of holiday do you prefer, eg beach, ski resort, countryside?

Table 6 gives an indication of existing timeshare owners' preference towards the number of bedrooms.

TABLE 6
SIZE OF TIMESHARE UNIT PURCHASED BY PERCENTAGE OF
RESPONSES

Size	UK (%)	Canada (%)	US (%)	Aus (%)
Studio	5	30.8	16.7	0.6
1 bedroom	16	43.4	31.4	6.2
2 bedrooms	73	24.0	41.9	84.6
3 bedrooms or more	6	1.8	10.0	8.6

Obviously, the unit size will depend on how many there are in your family and whether your children will shortly leave home. More space is needed in regional resorts for example, where weather conditions restrict to some degree outdoor activities. Conversely, space is less important at ski resorts, where most of the holiday is spent on the slopes.

How many weeks do I need? Purchases at urban and regional resorts tend to be less than at destination resorts. Table 7 gives some indication of weeks purchased. It should be borne in mind that it does not reflect the intentions of future purchasers.

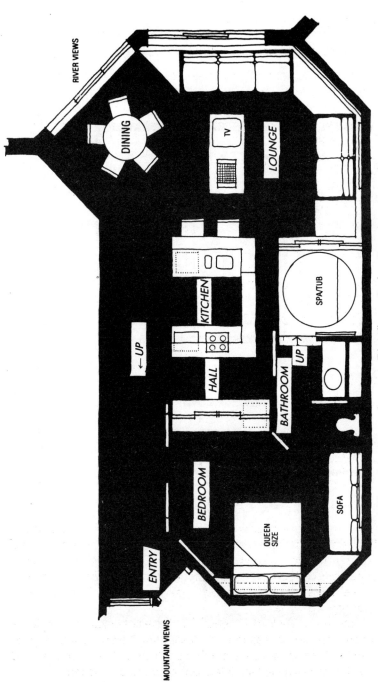

Fig 3 Typical apartment layout at Tiki Village, Surfers Paradise, Australia

The "Windermere" Lodge

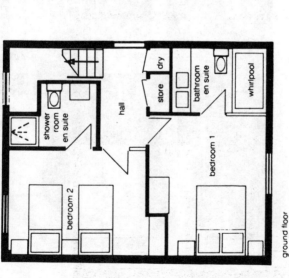

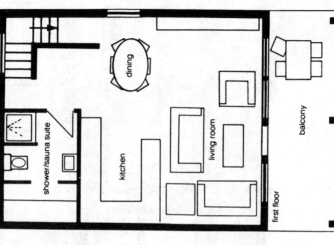

Fig 4 Two lodge designs at the Langdale Partnership, Cumbria:
'Windermere' sleeps six, 'Ullswater' sleeps eight

The "Ullswater" Lodge

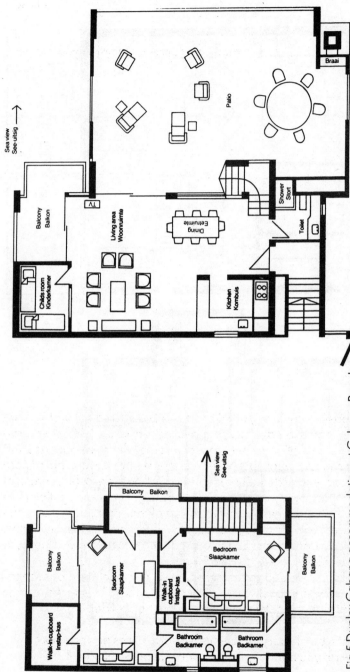

Fig 5 Duplex Cabana accommodation at Cabana Beach, South Africa, showing the upper level (left) and the lower level

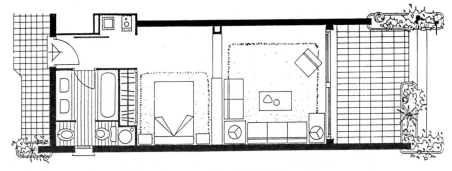

Fig 6 Studio suite at Pueblo Miraflores, Spain

TABLE 7
NUMBER OF WEEKS PURCHASED BY PERCENTAGE OF RESPONSES

No. of weeks	Australia (%)	UK (%)	Canada (%)	US (%)
1	39.2	43.0	53.0	17.0
2	39.2	38.0	34.0	44.0
3 and 4	16.5	17.0	11.0	24.0
5 or more	5.1	—	2.0	15.0
Average weeks	2.1	1.9	1.6	2.9

It is easy to visit a regional resort – only a short drive and you are there. It is also easy to visit a destination resort – either you are already on holiday in the general area or the developer has laid on a series of weekend inspection trips so that you can participate at a convenient date. By this time you will be more or less certain of what you want, inspection flight packages are negotiated at rock-bottom prices to justify the cost of the timeshares, and when you get there the developer usually offers some form of incentive, if you do decide to sign along the dotted line before you leave, to make the whole exercise worthwhile.

Having decided that timesharing is the ideal form of second-home ownership for you and your family, the following is a résumé of points to consider whilst doing your homework.

What type of sports and recreational facilities do you seek?
How do you normally travel when you go on holiday?

49

How many people would you plan for now?
How many people would you plan for in years to come?
At what time of year do you prefer to take your main holiday?
How do you prefer to spend the balance of the holiday entitlement?
With what types of people would you feel most relaxed when mixing?
What is the object of your holiday?
Would you feel relaxed about owning a second home in a country where you do not speak the language?

2. Your financial outlay
What is your normal maximum budget per week spent in either a hotel or rented accommodation?
Do you budget for an average spending allowance for food, drinks, entertainment and shopping trips?
Concessions?

3. Analysis of the resort
Is the location exactly what you want?
Is there a good package deal?
Does the resort management seem to operate efficiently and cost effectively?
Does the general atmosphere feel good?
Have you been provided with all the necessary assurances of occupancy?
Does the resort belong to one of the international exchange networks so that you can swap to another location if you want?
Do the resort calendar dates fit in with your normal holiday plans?
Check that the overall maintenance is well planned so that the property will remain in a good state of repair all year round.
Check if there are any local taxes that might further affect your budget.
Has a limit been placed on the number of persons who may occupy each different size of unit in order to prevent overcrowding and unnecessary wear and tear?
Does the basic cost of your timeshare adequately reflect the level of savings you have anticipated?
Are any rental and resale facilities available (you may just want to use one or other of these at some time in the future)?

Langdale, the Lake District, England

Is there a choice in methods of payments (a financed loan can sometimes afford you a better deal than cash, but check carefully)?

Have you read the small print? (The purchase agreement should clearly define your rights. The first page consists of the financial and membership details, but it is the reverse that needs careful reading as it contains all the inclusions, exclusions and restrictions. If you have your solicitor call the developer's solicitor, it can make all the difference and will not cost you the earth.)

What do owners complain about? Table 8 provides a useful guide to how existing timeshare owners from around the world rank their timeshares. Owners were asked whether they were very satisfied, satisfied, found purchase acceptable, were dissatisfied, or could not answer. The table gives the percentage of those who were actually dissatisfied.

TABLE 8
OWNERS' DISSATISFACTION

	UK %	US %
Size of unit	0	1.2
Kitchen facilities	0.8	1.3
Bathroom(s)	2.0	0.8
Storage space	2.9	2.2
Furnishings	0.4	1.1
Quality of construction	0.4	1.2
Cleanliness of unit	0.8	2.9
On-site recreation	23.4	3.0
Nearby recreation	8.2	1.9
Recreation for children	18.3	4.6
Restaurant(s)	13.4	5.6
Shopping	19.8	6.4
Attitude of management	5.5	4.3

3 Making Your Purchase

When you visit a timeshare resort it is normally with a view to becoming a potential owner. On arrival you will usually be ushered into a pleasantly appointed reception area with literature about the resort scattered around for you to read, enlarged photographs and/or posters on the walls, and a video recorder on which you can view a short presentation film of the resort and the exchange system in use. At this point you will be greeted by one of the sales consultants, who will take you on a grand tour and guide you through the whole process.

Generally speaking this is how it happens, but exact procedures depend entirely on a combination of methods used by a particular sales team and the size of the resort. For example, some resorts are so large and have so many visitors that a separate cinema-style room is used for organised video presentations at specific times to groups of between ten and twenty people. The actual tour is nearly always a strictly personal matter – just you, your partner and/or family, and the sales consultant.

The object of a resort tour is to show exactly what is available, how the units are designed, furnished and equipped, and what you will have in the way of on-site amenities. You will then have a far better understanding of what you will be getting for your money, both in terms of the once-only payment for whichever unit, week(s) and season(s) you choose, and what to expect when it comes to the annual maintenance fees.

Before you set off on the tour, you will probably spend some time chatting with your consultant – probably over a cup of coffee – so that you can get acquainted and have a chance to explain what you are looking for. During the tour itself you will be too busy listening and looking to say much, but do try to respond openly and honestly. A consultant cannot hope to learn everything about you in the short space of an hour or two, although most of them are well versed in human psychology! Their job is to try and sell you a holiday timeshare – obviously, since their livelihood is earned from commissions on sales. But take a resort where there is a particularly wide price range due to the number of unit types available; it is pointless spending too much time looking at apartments when you have set your heart on a villa. That is to say, you should try to state your preference clearly, whilst leaving your options open in case the consultant should come up with a more attractive alternative you had not thought about.

Whilst you are being taken around the show units, do look carefully at everything. This is when it pays to keep an open mind because you really should buy the best you can afford, and it is your consultant's job to help you find that which is most suitable to your needs.

Once the tour is over you will be taken back to a private office or area for further discussions and the moment of decision. This part of the operation seldom takes five minutes; custom therefore dictates that refreshments are offered, giving you breathing space to assemble your thoughts. If you plan to go ahead immediately with signing along the dotted line, then whatever form the transaction will take must be decided and the papers drawn up.

In very large resorts the financial transactions are completed by a special department set up specifically for the purpose – rather like opening an account at a major store. Otherwise your consultant will handle the matter.

If you are not prepared to make a decision, you may find that the consultant will not initially take no for an answer. His job is to convince you to purchase and, as he has been speaking to an average of two to three couples per day, he will, in most cases, have an answer to your reasons for not purchasing. However, do not be intimidated. Should you find yourself in a situation where the sales consultant or his manager is exerting pressure on you, tell him you are not prepared to make a decision today. Remember, he knows that the chance of your returning is less than five per cent so he will endeavour to get a financial commitment from you no matter how small.

Within the realm of sales psychology there are only two reasons that cannot be argued why a person will not make a commitment whether it be for a timeshare, car or any other consumer product. He either cannot afford it or he does not have use for it. If you suggest any other reason, the sales consultant will, most likely, have an answer to your objections.

Should you be confronted, in your opinion, with excessive sales pressure, do not be intimidated and do not offer objections that are not true. Explain your position and thank the consultant for his time and depart. Do not attempt to convince him of your point of view as your interests are no longer his interest. (Most professional companies adopt a purchaser's control sheet that reviews a client's understanding of what he has purchased. See Fig 7.)

Financial Considerations

Before you decide on what to purchase, review your financial limitations. The timeshare units vary greatly in price. A resort at the beginning of its operations will have more advantageous prices than a more mature resort. Likewise, a resort which offers substantial on-site facilities will have included some of these costs into the timeshare purchase price.

Prices also vary by size of unit and time of year. The price difference in a resort, however, like Marbella with its year-round season and golf opportunities, will vary less than the equivalent resort on the Costa Brava. Table 9 gives the likely price ranges at the time of writing.

TABLE 9
TIMESHARE PRICE RANGES IN POUNDS STERLING

Unit Size	High Season	Mid Season	Low Season
Apartments			
Studio	5,000	2,000	750
1 bedroom	7,000	3,000	1,000
2 bedroom	8,500	3,500	1,750
3 bedroom	10,000+	5,000	2,500
Villas			
1 bedroom	6,000	3,000	750
2 bedroom	9,000	4,000	2,000
3 bedroom	9,000	4,000	2,500
4 bedroom	10,000+	5,000	2,750

The above table should only be used as a guide because, as we discussed previously, prices do vary by resort for similar size units and are particularly relative to the on-site amenities available.

HOLIDAY OWNERSHIP EXCHANGE

48 LEICESTER SQUARE, LONDON WC2H 7LT. Tel: 01-839 7161

MEMORANDUM OF UNDERSTANDING
SUMMARY OF PURCHASE   MEMBERSHIP NUMBER :

		INITIALLED
1.	I UNDERSTAND my unit sleeps and exchanges for .... persons.	__ __
2.	I UNDERSTAND my current maintenance fee is £ ...... payable annually within 30 days of receipt of invoice.	__ __
3.	I UNDERSTAND my first year I.I. Membership is paid for and continuation of my Membership thereafter is optional.	__ __ __
4.	I UNDERSTAND that subject to availability I can exchange my weeks through Interval International and there is a nominal exchange fee.	__ __
5.	I UNDERSTAND I can rent my week(s) personally or request it to be rented out through management in Clube Praia Da Oura for a 20% commission (an additional 10% may be charged if rented through a travel agency) and that there is no absolute guarantee of rental by Clube Praia Da Oura.	__ __
6.	I UNDERSTAND I can sell my week(s) through any Estate Agency or Resale Agency any time, without prior approval of Clube Praia Da Oura, for any price, and that Clube Praia Da Oura will not commence it's resale programme until the existing inventory is sold.	__ __
7.	I WAS NOT coerced or high pressured to enter into this contract, and I have purchased of my own free will, because of the benefits this programme offers.	__ __
8.	I UNDERSTAND that this contract will be binding on both parties (Purchaser and Seller) at the time of signing and that the deposit is non-refundable and that neither party has a rescission period.	__ __
9.	I UNDERSTAND I have an uninterrupted right of ownership in Clube Praia Da Oura up to the year 2011 A.D. provided my annual maintenance fees are remitted in accordance with the rules in my contract and all payments are current if financed.	__ __
10.	I HAVE received a copy of:- (A) Clube Praia Da Oura Contract. (B) Investment Agreement. (C) Rules regarding the rights of Timeshare Occupancy. (D) Copy of Memorandum of Understanding.	__ __

Should you have any questions concerning your membership or any queries
concerning Interval International, contact the Membership Co-Ordinator,
Richard Dunning on 01=839=7161.

** WELCOME TO CLUBE PRAIA DA OURA **

MEMBER _____   MEMBER _____

WITNESS _____   WITNESS _____

_____
          HONDAWAY LIMITED   F. App 56
                                                  30.09.86

INTERNATIONAL
AWARD TO TOURIST
AND HOTEL INDUSTRY

Fig 7

57

When you have decided to purchase, consider the alternatives between cash and financed schemes. While many of us prefer to pay cash, with timeshare we are purchasing future holidays. On the assumption that we do take regular holidays, then the timeshare purchase price on a financed basis should roughly equate to what we spend on holidays each year (although with an increased level of luxury).

There are a number of finance packages available to assist you with your purchase. You will find that unsecured loans offered by the resort tend to be the most expensive. On balance, many timeshare owners have arranged their purchases with a bank loan.

Should the amount be too large or the monthly repayments too high, there are other programmes available which combine a second charge on your home and, coupled with an insurance endowment policy, effectively pay off the loan after a ten- or fifteen-year period.

Be careful not to over-extend yourself financially. One option is to purchase one week at a floating-time resort and then top it up with a second week later on. As they are both floating time, you may combine them for a future two-week holiday. Do not purchase weeks in a period which you do not intend to use, relying on your ability to exchange your weeks. Remember, exchange is a function of demand, the lower the demand the lower the opportunity to make a successful exchange. We will discuss this matter later, in Chapter 5. However, for the moment, suffice it to say that you should only purchase that time of year when you normally go on holiday.

If you find that you are unable to afford the weeks you want, talk it over with the sales consultant. He may well have a way to help with your financing requirements. After all, he is in the business to make sales and in most cases he will be happy to seek a workable payment formula to fit your particular needs.

The Sales Documents

At this point the most important document is the purchase agreement. It is a legally drawn up piece of paper, numbered and in duplicate or triplicate, which commits you to the purchase of whatever you have decided on, upon signature of your acceptance of the terms and conditions of the said agreement. This will include the constitution of the club or leasehold and the time limits for completion of payment.

But what if I do not want to purchase today? you may say. At this stage in our discussion, let us talk a little more about saying no. It is quite possible and logical that for a variety of reasons you do not wish to purchase on your first visit to the resort. You may not want to make a decision immediately because of other commitments which you have to make first, for example a new car or that extension to the house.

The sales consultant will do his best to secure your commitment on your first visit. He knows that there is an emotional factor in your decision, and he will do his best to exploit this. It is the same thing when buying a car. While a Metro will get you around it is much more pleasant to do so in a BMW. The same emotional process applies to any luxury consumer item. Do you really need a Rolex watch when a Timex would serve as well? These decisions are made on the spot as our emotional level will quickly drop when we depart from the scene. Therefore, your sales consultant will endeavour to secure your commitment right then and there. Surprisingly, the consultant's perseverance is often subsequently praised by the new timeshare owner who knows that without the consultant's efforts, he would not have purchased and therefore not have enjoyed the many benefits of timesharing.

For the above reasons, he will often offer you an inducement if you purchase on your first visit. He may offer you a ten to twenty per cent reduction on the price, a free first year's maintenance week or a round-trip air fare to the resort. These are all designed to commit you to a decision and at the same time reduce the administrative overheads for processing your transaction. Most consultants show the resort to two or three families per day. If you do not purchase but wish to return another time, the consultant will be obliged to reduce his income potential by one third to one half during the day you return as he will not be able to show the same number of families around the resort. Remember, time is money.

If you decide not to go ahead, do not be convinced otherwise. If you have an honest objection, explain it to the consultant. In most cases, a small non-refundable deposit will hold the timeshare week(s) for you until you can make your final decision.

But what happens if I purchase and subsequently realise I

cannot afford it? Purchasing a timeshare is like any other transaction. When contracts are exchanged, the transaction is completed. Should one party wish to withdraw at a later date, there is no obligation on the other party, unless previously agreed to in writing, to agree to dissolve the contract.

Lawyers call it *caveat emptor*, or 'let the buyer beware'. It is most important that you know what you are signing and what you are committing yourself to. Once you have signed, you are legally committed. The developer is sensitive to cancellations as it is a costly exercise to get interested buyers to the site. He not only must cover the marketing costs of getting you to the site (often £40 or more per couple) but also the cost of bringing others to the site who did not purchase. If we assume that one out of five people purchase then his cost per sale for lead generation is £200 (5 × 4).

Therefore, a cancellation request is an expensive business for him.

Many developers use a purchasers' checklist to review the salient points of the agreement with you after you have completed the purchase. It is their way of making sure that you understand the terms and conditions.

If you find that after you have purchased your timeshare, you cannot complete the agreement for whatever reason, do discuss it with your consultant or developer. Do not expect your money to be returned on the spot. However, if you can show him that you cannot complete for reasons outside your control, ie loss of employment rather than just a change of mind, he may be sympathetic and allow you to withdraw. He will, in most cases, seek a handling fee to defray his time and expenses made on your behalf.

Should you subsequently believe you have been misled, bring this to the immediate attention of the developer. If you are not satisfied write to the British Property Timeshare Association (see Useful Addresses section) which has a consumer protection committee to assist in resolving disputes of this nature.

Methods of Payment

Until fairly recently in Great Britain and Europe, the purchase of a timeshare meant a cash transaction, unless, of course, you were lucky enough to have a sympathetic bank manager. The next progression still involved the sympathetic bank manager, but this time at the behest of a developer frantically scouring around to boost his sales and help any would-be owners into the bargain. It was not an ideal arrangement – the loans were for specific resorts only, and the banks, acting as trustees, found themselves liable in cases of default.

The first finance house in the United Kingdom to show any sign of interest was Security Pacific Finance & Trust Ltd, an American organisation. Again it was not the best of arrangements but it was a step in the right direction. Today the variations available and flexibility of the schemes being offered are much greater.

Cash Purchases

When buying your timeshare a cash purchase is a simple transaction. You make a down payment, which is normally about twenty per cent of the agreed purchase price, and full settlement is due within a period of thirty days, upon which you are issued with your rights to occupy in respect of each week you have bought. The only real problem that could arise is if you decide to buy whilst already on holiday and, because you are abroad, you find yourself without a cheque book and sufficient ready cash. In such circumstances most resorts are prepared to accept a lower deposit or they are able to help you out in some other way such as holding the unit until you can return the following day to complete the papers.

Financed Loan Purchases

A timeshare transaction using a financed-loan method of payment is only more complicated in that you have to decide the best terms to suit your personal circumstances.

Financed loans can be secured or unsecured. Some offer built-in life assurance; others offer a money-back scheme at the end of the loan term (see Fig 8). Generally speaking, the maximum term for a holiday timeshare loan is, at present, fifteen years. The great pity is that you cannot walk into your building society's local office and take out a mortgage for a holiday timeshare, although one would imagine that the day is not far off. Your limitation is the number of schemes being offered by your chosen resort, but it is in their best interests to provide the best deal available to them.

A LIFETIME OF AFFORDABLE LUXURY HOLIDAYS

FOR BRITISH HOUSEOWNERS

10 YEAR CASH-BACK
LOAN SAVINGS SCHEME

The Cash-Back Scheme combines a Holiday Ownership Loan with a Savings Plan over 10 years, which will repay your loan in full and also leave you with a worthwhile tax-free lump sum.

YOU GET:
- **100% Holiday Ownership Loan Facility**
- **Guaranteed Repayment of your loan after 10 years**
- **Plus a tax-free lump sum for you**
- **Immediate life insurance cover built-in**

MONTHLY INSTALMENT CALCULATOR
Fixed term of agreement 120 months – arranged in multiples of £500
Monthly Interest Rate 1.21% (variable 15.6% APR)

| LOAN AMOUNT | MONTHLY OUTLAY | | | GUARANTEED HOLIDAY LOAN REPAID | | ESTIMATED CASH-BACK TAX-FREE SUM |
	PREMIUM	INTEREST	TOTAL			
£2,500	£25.00	£30.21	£ 55.21	**£2,500**	+	**£2,893**
3,000	30.00	36.24	66.24	**3,000**	+	**3,472**
3,500	35.00	42.29	77.29	**3,500**	+	**4,051**
4,000	40.00	48.33	88.33	**4,000**	+	**4,629**
4,500	45.00	54.38	99.38	**4,500**	+	**5,208**
5,000	50.00	60.42	110.42	**5,000**	+	**5,786**
5,500	55.00	66.46	121.46	**5,500**	+	**6,365**
6,000	60.00	72.50	132.50	**6,000**	+	**6,944**
6,500	65.00	78.54	143.54	**6,500**	+	**7,523**
7,000	70.00	84.58	154.58	**7,000**	+	**8,102**
7,500	75.00	90.63	165.63	**7,500**	+	**8,680**
8,000	80.00	96.67	176.67	**8,000**	+	**9,259**

Fig 8

62

Once you have signed up for your loan it does not mean that immediately you become the owner of the unit week(s) on the purchase agreement. First of all your documents must be submitted to the loan company for a credit rating and their acceptance – a process which takes around two to three weeks. Once you have been accepted you will be issued with the relevant title deed/membership certificate in respect of your purchase.

Cancellations and Refunds

One clause in the purchase agreement which should be carefully noted concerns whether or not a cooling-off period is allowed for. That is to say, does the developer allow you a number of days'grace during which you may change your mind and cancel any documents without forfeiting your deposit?

There is no hard-and-fast rule. Increasingly, developers allow a five- to fourteen-day period during which time you have the option to rescind your undertaking and get your deposit back; others do not even entertain the idea. None is under any obligation unless your purchase is financed.

Very much the same set of rules apply once you have taken out a loan to buy your timeshare through a finance house. Under the terms of the 1974 Consumer Credit Act they are not obliged to provide a cooling-off period where you sign your purchase agreement on site. Remember, if you seek a financed loan when buying a car you do not get the option to back out once you have signed on the dotted line.

Despite what seem to be very stringent rules, exceptions have been known to be made in cases of genuine hardship (for example, in the case of redundancy, severe illness or a death involving one of the parties to the contract). The trustees or the finance houses are usually most sympathetic in such circumstances and will react helpfully to explanatory letters backed by suitable corroboration of the facts. However, you cannot rely on this.

After-Sales Services

Once you have made your timeshare purchase and until all the various documents have been completed and exchanged hands, it is always helpful to know that you have a point of contact in case any queries arise on either side. (It is worth confirming this before you buy.)

When you buy in Great Britain the resorts have their own staff whose job it is to carry on from where the sales consultants left off. It is a different matter for purchases made outside the country – the thought of trying to communicate from afar where you have little or no knowledge of the language can prove daunting. Fortunately, the majority of European timeshare developers have a very high percentage of British owners or prospective owners, so you will find that many have some form of representation in Britain to maintain the thread of continuity. In fact, where there is a large organisation behind your resort's activities, you will find it of comfort to note that this continuity stretches far beyond the exchange of documents period, in that they will collect your annual maintenance fees and generally act as a point of contact between you and your resort for a great many other reasons.

4 Resort Management

Now that you have completed your timeshare purchase, your next concern is to ensure that your unit will be properly maintained in future years.

If you are fortunate to own your own home, you accept full management responsibility yourself and maintain its cleanliness, refurbish where and when necessary, and pay the various utility bills, insurance and property taxes. If you are a tenant, usually these responsibilities are not entirely yours.

As a timeshare owner, the management of your apartment is usually passed on to a management company which is employed by the collective timeshare owners at the resort. A similar arrangement would be that of the operation of a hotel or self-catering holiday property. After all, a timeshare project is equivalent to a hotel with guaranteed year-round occupancy.

The one fundamental difference of course is that, in most timeshare instances, the owners control the management company and, most important, have the right to dismiss them.

So how does it work? The management company is usually established at the outset by the developer. The developer's concern is to provide a high level of upkeep during the selling cycle.

If you have purchased into a large mixed-use complex whereby the developer has other commercial interests, such as hotels, self-catering rentals, restaurants and bars, you will usually find that he will also have an interest in the timeshare management company.

On the other hand, if you have purchased into a purpose-built timeshare resort with no permanent developer interests, you may well find that you and your co-owners control the management company entirely once the selling cycle is complete.

The developer will normally wish to retain control over the management company during the selling cycle as he is interested in maintaining standards during this time. He will usually accomplish this with a management contract. The sensible developer will never look at the management company as a profit centre and therefore there is little reason for a timeshare owner to do so either.

The objective of the developer is usually to ensure that he leaves himself no future liability upon completion of the selling cycle. Therefore, if the organisation of the development is structured properly, any profits are ploughed into the owners' account and the developer's liability is limited to the bare minimum, such as air space, fixtures and fittings and wall coverings.

You should always make sure at the outset that you and the other owners have sufficient powers to replace the existing management, except in those remote instances where your rights to occupy are limited in time and your annual charge is predetermined.

You will find in most cases that there exists an owners' association which will either have voting control of the management shares or voting control of the management company's board of directors. If this is not the case, beware!

Maintenance Fees

The management company is responsible for managing the day-to-day affairs of the resort, maintaining the units and common areas, replacing worn out and damaged items, paying the utility bills, insurance and property taxes, and controlling the access to the units and general security of the resort.

For these services, management will estimate the costs. To this lump sum they will add perhaps ten to fifteen per cent for their fees and then divide the sum total in proportion to the different type of units, based upon a sliding scale, allocating a fair proportion of costs to each size of unit. So, if you own a two-bedroom apartment, you would expect to have higher charges than your neighbour who owns a studio.

The management then divides the total allocated to each size apartment by the total number of weeks in order to arrive at an amount per week per apartment.

Let us look at this in practice. XYZ resort has a total budget for next year for operating costs and allowance for replacements of fixtures and furnishings of £158,750. The allocation per unit is then calculated and divided by the number of weeks. In the example

TABLE 10
XYZ RESORT: CALCULATION OF THE MAINTENANCE CHARGE

Unit Size	Budget Allocation £	No. of Units	Total No. of Weeks (No. of units x 50)	Maintenance Fee per Week (Budget allocation ÷ no. of weeks) £
2 bedrooms	63,750	15	750	85
1 bedroom	70,000	20	1,000	70
Studio	25,000	10	500	50
Total	158,750	45	2,250	

we use fifty weeks as two weeks are excluded for annual maintenance.

Most management companies use a single annual billing system which usually requests the owners to pay the following year's management charge by the first day of the year. In this manner, the billing cost is kept to a minimum. Management knows immediately who is delinquent and if necessary will take steps on your behalf to preclude access to any owners who have not contributed their share of the costs.

Management fees are usually assessed according to one of two systems, either single tier or two tier.

The assessment in the former case is the sum total of the annual expenses and charges divided by the number of units, with an allowance against the actual size of the units. You may find that your resort will charge you separately for energy costs. This is accomplished through the use of individual meters. While you may feel this is a bit cumbersome, it does save on expense as each one is directly responsible for their own energy costs.

Do not be surprised however if you purchase into a highly seasonal resort and find that the maintenance fee varies by time of year for the same unit. This is often the case where there are large common areas which need heating during the winter months, for example at a ski resort. This is the two-tier system.

In other instances the owner may be assessed against actual use of the unit. Developments employing this system tend to fall into the mixed hotel/timeshare schemes where the owner's unit is constantly pooled into a collective rental scheme. While the nature of the development is timesharing, the lease usually runs for less than twenty-five years – often as low as ten years – and amounts to more of a prepaid rental programme where the initial payment constitutes a premium for discount on future rentals. The annual fee covers both management costs and rent.

Maintenance fees from the management company's point of view will be discussed later in the chapter.

Management Responsibilities

Holiday ownership schemes require a completely different sort of management from any other type of property, as they are a blend of traditional personal property ownership and hotel-type occupancy. The areas of responsibility fall into the following categories.

Occupancy
There is a continuous and high level of occupancy throughout the year around the units, the facilities, and the service areas, changing every one to two weeks. This can cause problems which would not arise in other types of property.

Traffic Flow
Your management needs to be able to provide a twenty-four-hour service for processing the incoming and outgoing owners. This not only involves the handing over of keys, but also unit inventory control, the assessment of charges such as electricity and telephones and other extras, and the provision of storage facilities for each incoming owner.

Changeovers
Timeshare schemes in the United Kingdom, United States, Canada, and Australia tend to use a fixed day for occupancy turnover. Saturday is the most usual, with check out before 10am and check in after 4pm. France, Italy and Spain, and in many cases South Africa, fixed dates rather than days are used.

Places that rely almost solely on air transport, such as Malta, the Canary and Balearic Islands, and Scandinavia to some extent, use floating days, to coincide with the charter flights whose permits are negotiated annually. As airlines usually have high weekend bookings for holiday destinations they are able to offer more advantageous prices on certain weekdays. As a result, many schemes fix their check-in and check-out days to coincide with the availability of cut-price fares.

Some large timeshare resorts stagger the check-in/check-out days by villa numbers, floor levels, or some such. An alternative is to roll over the departure and entry days. For example, depart Saturday and enter Sunday, but the problem here is the loss of one day's occupancy per owner, which is obviously not popular.

Damage and Breakages

When you arrive at your resort, you are usually given an inventory control form. It is your responsibility to review the contents of your unit, assess possible excessive wear and damage and return the completed form to the reception within twenty-four hours. As we are all owners in the collective sense, we tend to have a stronger interest than, say, the one-off rental. Your interest is to maintain the standard of the unit and the common parts. Should damage be done it is your obligation to report it and, after assessment, pay for its repair or replacement. Should you disagree with the amount charged there is usually a procedure for arbitration. If, on the other hand, the matter is not settled, then there is usually a procedure restricting your access to the unit until the matter has been resolved. There are very few instances of this as there usually exists a strong bond amongst the timeshare owners which overrides this problem.

Mixed Schemes

At properties where both timeshare units and traditional rentals are combined complicated situations can arise. Management companies must be able to understand the attitude of the timeshare occupants, who have a sense of ownership and belonging unlike the rental guests whose interests are limited only to their daily enjoyment of a single holiday. With mixed schemes, pilfering from the units can be a problem due to the availability of odds and ends that are easily disposable such as cutlery and glassware.

Defaulters

Most owners pay their annual assessment charges in accordance with their contractual requirements. However, due to the numbers involved, a definitive and well explained procedure for ensuring prompt payment and a legal protection against default must be established. The management company must have the right in case of default either to rent out the unit or to repossess it.

It is rare that an owner attempts to overstay the allocated time, but here again a set and legalised system should be set up lest such a situation arise.

Floating Time

An ever increasing number of timeshare schemes are using floating time-periods, thereby allowing greater flexibility for their owners. The allocation of floating time increases the burden on the management company and therefore it is important that a very well planned reservations system is in existence.

Exchanges

Figures indicate that more than twenty-five per cent of all seasoned timeshare owners — that is to say persons who have been owners for three years or more — exchange once every three years. In order to process exchanges in an effective manner it is necessary in most cases to allocate this responsibility to one person. That person then will not only be in charge of incoming exchanges, but will also be thoroughly familiar with all the procedures of the firm to which the scheme is affiliated, in order to provide an efficient service to owners who may have questions as to how various aspects of the system work.

Resales

It has been a misconception in the industry that a timeshare, once sold, stays sold. The traditional argument that a combination of exchange and rental facilities satisfies every owner's needs is now realised to be a fallacy. It is estimated that any fully sold-out scheme will have upwards of ten to fifteen per cent of its occupants looking for resales annually.

There are many reasons why an owner may wish to resell. In most instances, he will turn to the management for help. And given this minimum ten-per-cent demand, it is up to the management company either to provide this service or to be able to refer enquiries on.

Your Management Company

The management company is there to protect your interests. Through your home owners' association, you will elect members to the management committee to supervise activities. Through the owners' committee and the general meetings, you will have the opportunity to express your concerns and anxieties and, indeed, if you and your co-owners feel strongly about it, to cancel the management contract.

The management company is run just like any other business. It provides its assigned services, and reports to its board, who in turn report to the shareholders or trustees acting on your behalf.

Most contracts last for three years. In practice, they tend to perpetuate themselves, as a close working relationship develops between the owners and management staff.

Your voting rights as an owner are usually in proportion to the number of weeks owned. It is quite normal to appoint a proxy for management meetings if you are unable to attend. In the case of those owning units in hotels, it is usually neither feasible nor practicable to have such rights. In these instances there should be a written management agreement to the timeshare owners which clearly defines the extent of the services and their costings.

The initial responsibility of setting up the management company lies with the developer and there are generally three basic ways in which it can be done:

1. A separate company may be formed and taken over by the purchasers upon completion of the project.
2. The developer himself may continue to manage the project using an independent firm of auditors to report to the purchaser.
3. The developer may sign a contract with an outside professional firm, who will take over the running.

In all cases the management company must prepare budgets and project its operating costs. These costs are then apportioned among the owners pro rata, when payment is due, usually before the date of entry. In those rare cases of non-payment, the user is normally barred from the unit until payment has been met in full. There are various legal ways to restrict and regain entry depending on the laws of the land where you purchase your timeshare.

The maintenance charge is somewhat similar to paying municipal rates in that the monies are allocated to various services. As we shall shortly explain in greater detail, there is firstly the cost of the day-to-day running which includes insurance, tax and staff salaries, and management profit in the case of a third party concern. Secondly there is a fund to be topped up annually to provide for the refurbishment of the units every four to six years. Lastly there is a similar fund to provide for any major future expenses such as boiler replacement or renewal of the air-conditioning unit. Security is also a special expense. Apartment keys are usually changed periodically, and modern systems, such as used in some of the bigger hotel chains, for example, the use of computerised and magnetised cards permitting a constant change of locking mechanisms, are becoming increasingly popular at timeshare resorts.

The owners' association usually delegates the following powers to the management:

1. To make rules and regulations from time to time.
2. To schedule owners' meetings.
3. To contract and dismiss management staff.
4. To assess and levy both regular and special charges.
5. To control management personnel and monitor the operation of the project.
6. To enter any unit during reasonable hours for the purposes of maintenance, repairs or replacements, or emergencies.
7. To enforce the terms and conditions pertaining to apartment occupancy documents.
8. To make owner assessments.
9. To enforce liens on non-payment of charges and have powers to foreclose for costs plus legal fees and so on.
10. To withhold unit from defaulter and rent out in interim.
11. To enforce occupancy restrictions to insure against nuisances and disturbances.
12. To make legal procedures to guard against owners staying beyond their departure date.
13. To monitor specific provisions for developer to turn over control to owners' association.
14. To monitor orderly termination of life of project.
15. To reserve unit requirements for the exchange company.

16. To guarantee maintenance by developer during selling cycle.
17. To define responsibilities in mixed-use plans.
18. To decide when common areas may be used and by whom.

The management company will usually build up its costs in the following way.

1. Unit Operating Costs

The annual cost of cleaning, linen changes, ordinary wear and tear, allowance for breakages, taxes and utility charges are estimated. Generally, resorts provide a twice-a-week linen change and a once-a-week cleaning service. There will usually be an amount allocated to cover a package of coffee, tea, milk, rolls, butter, jam and cereal to get you through breakfast the day after you arrive. You may also find flowers and a bottle of wine awaiting your arrival.

2. Unit Replacement and Refurbishment Costs

Management will determine the normal life expectancy of the fixtures, furnishings and decoration and create a fund to replace these when the need arises. In most cases, repainting is done every two to three years, replacement of curtains and furniture every five years and kitchen fixtures every eight to ten years.

3. Common Areas – Operating, Replacement and Refurbishment Costs

Similar allocations are made as in 1 and 2 above to assess the costs of the common areas, which include walkways, lifts, common rooms and gardens. The costs will vary by project, for example some may have golf courses or tennis courts, others vast tracts of ground to be landscaped, others saunas, pools and discotheques or clubs.

It is very important to the owner to know exactly how the charges are apportioned. A promoter should set up the management operation as a separate body so that each charge can be recorded individually and an annual breakdown provided in detailed form to present to the owners. The management books should also be available for general inspection.

4. Administration Expenses

Administration and reception expenses are budgeted and entered into the calculations.

5. Management Fees

Management usually charges a fee based upon a minimum flat amount plus a percentage of operating costs, or a straight percentage, usually about fifteen per cent, for its services.

How are you protected against unscrupulous cost allocations? The management entity is operating within guidelines established from the outset by the legal documentation which created the timeshare resort. The terms and conditions will determine the limits of responsibility and the method of assessing the maintenance fees and its own fees. This is your main protection.

The next layer of protection is the appointment of your representative to the management's board or supervisory committee. You are then in a position to question the day-to-day operation and query any areas of concern.

Management is charged to provide the owners with a year-end financial report and estimated budget for the following year. Thus, through the annual auditing of these accounts, you are protected.

But what if something goes wrong? At time of purchase you will receive a legal documentation giving your rights to occupy. Included with this documentation is a covenant binding all the owners together and committing you to respect certain conditions. These regulations are usually known as user or owners' rules and regulations. It sets out all the little details that hopefully create a feeling of harmony each time you use your timeshare. (Many resorts forbid pets, not necessarily to penalise the owner but to protect the next owner who may be allergic to animal hair. Often there are restrictions on noise after certain hours, the hanging out of washing or sticking signs on windows.) These restrictions are designed to protect your privacy and comfort and to ensure that you have an enjoyable holiday. Other rules set out the structure and method of operation of the management company, the method of paying the annual maintenance fees, on-site charges, electricity and telephone, and check-in and check-out times. These rules have been developed to protect you should something go amiss, they should have a system for redress.

Should an owner fail to live up to his responsibilities then he must pay the consequences. This could mean he may have to make compensation or be forbidden entry to his unit. On the other hand, should management not live up to their responsibilities then the owners' association has the right to ask them to stand down and, if need be, take legal action.

Timeshare resorts, by their very nature, have built-in protection. During the selling cycle, the developer is most anxious to foster an efficient management company as his interests are directly concerned with maintaining a high standard. Towards the close of the selling cycle, there will be opportunity for the new management company to settle down and for the owners' association to assume control. In most cases, a timeshare resort needs two to five years to sell out. During this time the budgets can be accurately determined from actual operating costs, thereby affording the owners a realistic and tested maintenance fee at project completion.

Of course, there can be surprises. A resort may not accrue sufficient reserves for replacement of its fixtures and furnishings, which will result in a surcharge on future maintenance fees. This is the exception rather than the rule. As the timeshare industry grows there is a greater flow of statistical information which increases the developer's and the management company's ability to forecast the costs accurately.

5 The Exchange Organisations

Exchanging homes is nothing new. If fact, it has been a traditional source of inexpensive holidays for educational establishments and other groups or individuals throughout the world for many years. Firms like Home Interchange and Homeswap publish annual listings of people interested in swapping their home for another. Lists are circulated among interested parties who make direct contact with a view to swapping homes among themselves. It has also become an accepted and a well established cost-effective way for teachers to travel abroad for extended periods during the long school and university holidays.

Home exchanges, or one-to-one swaps, are restrictive in the sense that two families must be able to agree on simple details such as where and when. While this is not an insurmountable problem where there are standard holiday patterns, it does not provide the solution to a universal exchange system.

However, the world timeshare industry took a giant step forward in the 1970s with the advent of the exchange organisation. Before this innovative move, the chief objection to timesharing was that a purchaser had no option but to return to the same place year after year unless he was able to rent his unit.

How They Started

Originally holiday timeshare was considered by many to be a 'poor man's second home', something to buy if you could not afford to purchase a second home outright. The units usually reflected it too, with sparse furniture and limited space. The Americans changed that. During the property crisis in the early '70s a number of United States developers started to sell luxury apartment buildings on a timeshare basis. To their pleasant surprise, the units started to sell. More and more developers sensed a new property opportunity and an increasing number of projects entered the market place.

It was not long before the developers realised that their product was no longer 'classic' property, that is, purchased for investment and/or retirement, but, rather, was viewed by the purchaser as a holiday package, a means to guarantee future holidays at today's prices.

However, one problem continued to nag the developers and that was, how to sell a holiday which required the owners to return year after year at the same time to the same place.

Unbeknown to the timeshare developers at this time a small family company called Resort Condominiums International (RCI) based in Indianapolis, Indiana, had started up in 1974 providing exchange services for second-home owners. Founded by Christel and Jon DeHaan, the company was finding it increasingly difficult to balance its books as their subscription base and volume of exchanges were limited. Jon DeHaan, hearing of the holiday timeshare concept, realised that this might be a solution to his problem. After all, twenty-five subscribers per unit on a timeshare basis beats one subscriber, even on a sole ownership basis.

The developers were equally enthusiastic, as Chris and Jon's exchange company offered them the first opportunity to sell their timeshares as holiday packages as distinct from property packages.

The very first company to concentrate wholly on the timeshare exchange had been Holiday Exchange Club Ltd founded by the author in London in 1973. In 1977 it merged with RCI to create the first multinational exchange system.

RCI had started in 1974 with four buildings in various resort centres in the USA. Today more than 1,200 resorts in fifty-five countries are affiliated and more than half a million timeshare owners are RCI members. During 1985 RCI completed 185,097 exchanges.

Today, there are two major independent exchange companies, RCI, still based in Indianapolis and Interval International (II) based in Miami, founded in 1975 and headed by Mario Rodriquez and Ken Knight. Both of these companies employ vetting procedures covering the quality of the resort and its units, and verify the legal documentation and the commercial viability of the scheme.

Recently, a number of new exchange companies have started up. Unlike RCI and II, these companies cater more for the individual rather than a resort as a whole. Many timeshare owners belong to more than one exchange company. The pioneering efforts of, first, RCI and then II have created a viable industry, and an indication of the number of competitors, using various systems, which have appeared on the scene since 1980 is given below.

Firm	Founded
Holiday Exchange Club (HEC)	1973
Resort Condominiums International (RCI)	1974
Interval International (II)	1975
International Vacation Exchange (IVE)	1980
International Resort Exchange System (IRES)	1981
Vacation Horizons International (VHI)	1981
Universal Timeswap (UTS)	1981
Network One (Network 1)	1982
Exchange Network (EN)	1982
Travelex	1982
European Passport	1983
Eurex	1986

The assimilation of the exchange organisations into the timeshare industry has created a tremendous growth throughout the world. The table below illustrates this point.

TABLE 11
SUBSCRIBERS TO EXCHANGE ORGANISATIONS

Year End	II	RCI
1986*	250,000	750,000
1985	215,000	561,018
1984	171,414	473,328
1983	135,108	334,570**
1982	155,000	250,756
1981	120,000	170,919
1980	90,000	180,000
1979	50,000	70,901
1978	27,200	38,046
1977	10,500	17,891
1976	2,800	5,000
1975	n/a	1,600

* Estimated
** RCI/VHI merged in Ocober 1983

Exchange Systems in Practice

Affiliation procedures to the exchange organisations vary. However, both II and RCI have very stringent standards and requirements for the contractual arrangments with a promoter. A number of the new entrants offer exchanges on a freer, individual or non-contractual basis. The exchange company's contractual arrangement may or may not limit a promoter to processing all exchanges through the system.

TABLE 12
EXAMPLES OF EXCHANGE ORGANISATION CHARGES 1986

	II £	RCI £
Annual subscription fee	42	38
Exchange fee	42 (up to 2 wks)	38 (per wk)
Guest certificate	—	15 (per wk)
Re-enrolment fee	85	100

As part of the membership fee, each owner receives regular publications from the exchange organisation with up-to-date information on resorts available, new procedures, special fare deals and so on. Upon lapse of the automatic enrolment period, subscriptions are voluntary. However, a penalty is incurred for a lapse in membership and subsequent re-enrolment which is unattractive enough to make an owner think twice — otherwise most people would only subscribe for the year in which they chose to exchange.

Affiliation to one of the exchange companies is, for all intents and purposes, a prerequisite for new timeshare projects entering the marketplace.

As a buyer, the resort will automatically enrol you into the exchange company for one or more years depending upon the resort's enrolment policy. Your membership documents, which include your member's card, directory of resorts and the exchange forms, will be posted to you within three to six weeks after you have completed your purchase. As a member of the exchange company your timeshare ownership is now a passport to the world! A brief look at the table below will provide you with

INTERVAL INTERNATIONAL
The Quality Holiday Exchange Network ™

HOLIDAY EXCHANGE REQUEST
(Please print or type)

IMPORTANT: You must complete all parts of this form.
This request must be received at least 60 days prior to the date requested for exchanges to and from destinations within Europe, or 90 days in advance for exchanges to and from all other destinations. This request must be accompanied by the required exchange fee. £42 00

MEMBERSHIP INFORMATION

I.I. Membership Number ☐☐☐☐☐☐

Own Resort Code (3 letters) ☐☐☐   Own Resort Name ☐☐☐☐☐☐☐☐☐☐☐☐☐☐☐☐☐

Surname / Forename(s)

Name

Address

Town / County

Postcode / Country

Tel. No: Home ☐☐☐ STD Code   Business ☐☐☐ STD Code

EXCHANGE FEE

Please debit ☐ Access/Mastercard ☐ American Express ☐ Diners Club ☐ Visa

Expiry Date ☐☐☐☐   Card No. ☐☐☐☐☐☐☐☐☐☐☐☐☐☐☐☐

☐ Cheque enclosed for £ _____

HOME RESORT ACCOMMODATIONS – Enclose a Reservation Form for floating week(s)

Year to be Exchanged ☐☐

Type of Unit (Enter Right Code)
0-Studio 1-1 BR 2-2 BR
3-3 BR 7-Other 9-Hotel

Week No.	Dates Day/Month/Year		Type of Unit	Unit No.
1.	☐☐☐☐☐☐ to	☐☐☐☐☐☐	☐	☐☐☐☐☐
2.	☐☐☐☐☐☐ to	☐☐☐☐☐☐	☐	☐☐☐☐☐

EXCHANGE DESIRED

A valid request must include a combination of at least **four different area codes and time periods: one area and three time periods; two areas and two time periods; or three areas and one time period.** You may also request the **ONE** specific RESORT you most desire, located in your first-choice holiday area code.

Preferred Resort Code (3 letters) ☐☐☐

Resort Areas Desired – Do you have an area preference? ☐ Yes ☐ No
(Enter Holiday Area Code)

1. Area ☐☐☐ OR 2. Area ☐☐☐ OR 3. Area ☐☐☐ OR 4. Area ☐☐☐

Weeks Preferred – Do you have a date preference? ☐ Yes ☐ No
You may only request to travel prior to and/or inclusive of the dates you are relinquishing.

1. Week of ☐☐ ☐☐ ☐☐ (Day Month Year) OR 2. Week of ☐☐ ☐☐ ☐☐ (Day Month Year) OR

3. Week of ☐☐ ☐☐ ☐☐ (Day Month Year) OR 4. Week of ☐☐ ☐☐ ☐☐ (Day Month Year)

Number of People Travelling ☐ Adults ☐ Children under 12
The size of the unit received in exchange is determined by the number of people in your party.

The Terms and Conditions of Exchange have been read and it is understood that this Holiday Exchange Request is subject to such Terms and Conditions

MEMBER: _____ (Signature)   Date: _____

MEMBER: _____ (Signature)   Date: _____

This verifies that the week(s) relinquished has not been, nor will be, offered for rental or exchange through another service, unless written cancellation has been acknowledged by Interval.

Send the completed request form, with payment, to Worldex Europe, Gilmoore House, 57-61 Mortimer Street, London W1N 7TD UK

Fig 9

some idea of the scope and size of the operations of the two main exchange companies.

TABLE 13
II AND RCI WORLD TRADING 1985

	II	RCI
Resorts	500	1,143
Countries	30	54
Subscribers	215,000	561,018
Exchanges	38,000	185,097

The Spacebank Exchange

Spacebanking was introduced in 1974 by RCI. This system operates much like a bank account in that you make deposits and withdrawals of time.

Quite simply, an owner wishing to exchange 'deposits' his time in the spacebank and then 'withdraws' that time he wishes to use. These deposits and withdrawals are controlled by computer to provide an equal exchange. Exchange requests are coded by size of apartment/villa, number of bedrooms, time of year (whether high, middle or low). Exchanges are possible for the same size and occupancy or lower, and same time bands or down, but not up.

One obvious problem with the spacebank approach, as introduced by RCI, is the occasion when a simultaneous deposit and withdrawal are not effected. It *is* possible to lose one's deposit without any assurance of immediately obtaining a satisfactory withdrawal. However, RCI's computer is programmed to calculate in advance the probable availability of an exchange and the result is a high success rate of over ninety per cent in matching deposits with withdrawal requests.

To deposit a low-demand period against a request for a higher demand period will obviously meet with resistance. An example of this would be a September exchange of a two-bedroom luxury lodge in Scotland for a two-bedroom luxury villa in Marbella, Spain. At that time of year the demand for Scotland would be considerably less than that for Marbella.

To overcome these problems an accrual system is now in use. This allows owners who are unable to find a satisfactory exchange

– or indeed do not wish to exchange or use their units in a given year – to receive a credit for an equivalent number of weeks for the following year. A priority system is allocated to the owners, based upon the date of the original exchange request.

RCI also recently introduced a 'reverse' accrual exchange programme that enables the purchaser at a new resort, which may not be formally open at the time of purchase, to spacebank his next year's time and exchange it for a holiday at another resort during the current year.

RCI's tremendous growth has led to an imbalance in demand between North America and Europe. More North American members are looking for exchanges to Europe than the reverse. To get around this problem, they have introduced at the time of writing a two-for-one exchange programme for Europeans who own in European resorts. This programme is subject to annual renewal until the demand redresses itself. However, for the moment a European resident can deposit one week of time in a European resort and withdraw two weeks of time in a North American resort. Effectively, it doubles your holiday time or put another way, it reduces your timeshare holiday cost by fifty per cent each time you use the two-for-one programme.

The Linear Exchange

In 1975 II became the second exchange company to enter the fast-expanding market of timeshare exchange. They positioned their stance between the original one-to-one system and RCI's spacebank by deciding to link their deposits and withdrawals to a revolving circuit. In this way, until the circle was completed, an exchange could not be effected, thereby assuring an owner that he actually had somewhere to go before committing his time.

Unlike RCI, II has not adopted specific time bands to denote high, middle or low seasons. Instead, it matches demand patterns among its members as they vary. This system does provide greater flexibility than RCI's spacebank in that it 'locks' the deposit into the withdrawal without relying on the time of year. In certain cases it can be described as arbitrary, but, year round, it does let the demand probability provide the determining factor. Importantly, with the II system, in the event of an exchange not being effected, the member's home resort weeks are still available for the member's own use.

Both the major exchange companies have found it necessary initially to augment their available space through the use of a promoter's unsold units. This boosts their deposits before the deposits of their members.

The use of a promoter's unsold space assists exchange requests where, for instance, few, if any, owners are considering exchanging. High demand areas such as Acapulco and London can rarely be satisfied through normal exchange channels.

II has associated its name with the quality ratings of timeshare resorts with II Five Star and Interval 500 resort accolades. Resort owners within this category may inter-exchange among themselves to the exclusion of II affiliated resorts not designated within these categories, thereby providing a greater assurance of high-quality exchanges.

A number of promoters have created their own internal exchange systems, which may or may not be affiliated to the multinationals.

Internal Open-Pool Systems
Many resorts now offer an internal exchange service for their owners. The most effective of these systems are at resorts offering floating time because you are given the opportunity to select your time each year. Usually, your time frame will be limited to the seasonal band which you purchased, but many resorts offer interseasonal exchanges once owners have selected their week(s) within a seasonal band. So you may find that three months beforehand, the resort will entertain an interseasonal exchange request.

Resorts with fixed weeks tend to limit their internal exchanges to a listing service which enables owners to communicate among themselves and arrange private one-to-one swaps.

More recently, you will find that a number of resorts in different areas and, indeed, in different countries, are owned by one group. These multiple-resort operations are creating a new dimension to exchange by offering their owners quality control on resorts, priority for internal exchanges and the added benefit of the external exchange system.

The Hapimag System
One of the industry's pioneers, Hapimag, set up an internal

exchange system as an integral part of its structure. Incorporated as a joint stock company, it sells shares to the public and uses the proceeds to purchase apartments – and, more recently, entire buildings. The shareholders receive a number of points, depending on the extent of their acquisition, which in turn gives them certain priority rights to use the apartments within the system. Each apartment is allocated a specific number of points for each week of the year, which gives a higher rating for peak-season weeks.

As the industry grows, we will see increasing numbers of these multiple resorts with both their internal exchanges and affiliations with one of the major external exchange companies.

Each share certificate is allocated a fixed number of points. Thus, the more shares owned, the greater the surety one has in obtaining a specific time and place. To ensure equitable results, the computer programme has a built-in priority system, similar in some respects to those of RCI and II, whereby a shareholder who received his first request the previous year will have lower priority the following year.

Unlike the more traditional timeshare schemes, Hapimag shareholders own rights to use within a 'pool' rather than specific units. The only requirement is that they book by 1 January for summer-holiday resorts and by 1 July for winter-holiday centres. The priority points system gives a better chance of acquiring a first choice.

Hapimag's system has a distinct advantage over the multinationals' in that its entire space is available each year (around 1,500 villas/apartments at the time of writing). This obviously leads to a higher exchange success rate. It is also of particular appeal to timesharers who like to change their holiday resorts regularly.

The Holiday Property Bond System

A recent innovation on the Hapimag system has been developed by Holiday Property Bond (HPB), an Isle of Man insurance trust.

HPB has taken the next logical step by allocating part of the proceeds to gilt-edged investments as well as to property acquisition. The income derived from these investments enables the bond managers to cover the maintenance and refurbishment fees of the property together with the general administrative overheads; therefore, the bond holders, unlike other timeshare owners, are not called upon to pay any further annual charges once they have paid for the bond.

Japanese Timeshare Systems
Timesharing in Japan is run along similar lines to the Hapimag system, with the majority of projects operating a club membership system that conveys rights to occupy space from a pool of units (often hotel accommodation).

Optional Pool Systems
Most of the in-house exchange systems have tended to follow the more traditional timeshare schemes whereby rights of occupancy are conveyed to a particular unit for a particular period of time. There are certain variations where either the unit and/or the time may float. Owners then pool their time internally by placing their units into the exchange. In the United States, Fairfield Communities, the country's largest timeshare developer, based in Atlanta, Georgia, is an example of a large operator currently using this system. Called Fairshare exchange, it uses both an internal and an external exchange system through its affiliations with RCI.

Club Hotel, the largest timeshare operation in France and part of the Club Méditerranée group, offers its own internal service called La Clé de l'Echange (the exchange key). To date they have 32,000 owners and thirty-six resorts in France and one in the Canary Islands.

Using the optional pool system, the timeshare owners retain the decision to use the exchange when they want to with no danger of forfeiting their time. They also have the assurance of knowing where their home is each year, plus the advantage of low cost inter-resort exchanges having similar standards and uniform management.

A Few Hints on Making Exchanges

The major exchange organisations are very effective in providing an excellent exchange service. You should remember, however, that when you make your exchange request, it is based upon available space in the exchange system. For you to be successful, someone else will have had to give up their own time.

Your key to successful exchanges is to give the exchange company the widest latitude possible in both holiday dates and resorts. The greater the options the better chance you have of receiving your confirmation. Exchange companies cater for last-minute exchanges which can be made by telephone giving only a few days' notice. But remember, the closer to your intended departure date the less chance of obtaining what you request.

The exchange organisations have high confirmation rates, although this does not necessarily mean that each resort has the same exchange success rate. You must remember that the foundation of the exchange system is based on a series of priorities. A resort in, say, Marbella would have greater demand in the summer than in the winter. Conversely, a ski resort would have its greatest demand in the winter months. Likewise, a new resort recently opened would have less space than a resort that sold out several years ago – after all, most of us want to use our own units for one or two years before we consider exchanging.

Rule 1
Choose, where possible, mature resorts. The RCI directory has a code system showing the number of members at each resort. The greater the member base, the greater the chance of exchange. Also, look at the size of the resort. Obviously, the greater the number of units, the greater the opportunity of available exchange space.

Rule 2
Be flexible. Timeshare exchange is based on availability of space. It is not based upon a hotel reservation system. The greater the alternative resorts/locations and the time frames you propose in your exchange request, the greater the likelihood of receiving an acceptable exchange. Where possible choose areas rather than resorts and early and latest departure dates rather than specific dates.

Remember, someone must give up their time in order for you to use it!

Rule 3
The early bird catches the worm. Submit your exchange request

and donate your own space at the earliest date possible. The greater the time before your intended departure, the greater the probability of an acceptable exchange.

Rule 4

Are your forms properly completed? Have you enclosed your fees? Chat with any exchange official and you will hear countless stories about incomplete documentation. Be careful to read the instructions in detail. When in doubt contact the exchange company before submitting your forms. In addition, make sure your membership dues are paid up to date.

Recent Exchange Developments

In most timeshare surveys the exchange facility is rated either as the most important or second most important reason for purchasing.

The major exchange companies are continually enlarging their member services. You will find that they provide you with car-hire discounts, travel and insurance services and sometimes rental services should you wish not to use your timeshare at any time. It is now possible to obtain last-minute exchanges by telephone. (See Chapter 7 for more details.)

When you become a timeshare owner, your membership into the exchange system should be your passport to holidays throughout the world.

6 Consumer Protection

The industry is growing very rapidly at the time of writing. Among British residents it has grown from some 150 owners in 1975 to well over 80,000 at the present time. The rate of sales to British residents currently exceeds 2,000 families per month. When you look at the possible level of luxury, the exchange systems and the savings on future holidays it is not difficult to understand why the industry is growing so fast at the present time. Unfortunately, as with any rapidly growing industry, the pitfalls to the buyer and to the seller are not always evident. There are elements of risk which need to be understood.

Timesharing in Europe, with the exception of France and Portugal, has no specific legislative guidelines. It falls under existing property, credit and sales legislation. Timeshares are neither definable as a property nor holiday purchase and consequently prevailing property and holiday/travel legislation does not offer the timeshare purchaser the same degree of protection. Therefore, before you purchase, you should stand back and ask yourself a few questions concerning your prospective timeshare interest.

Questions to Ask

1. Are your rights to occupy secure? Before signing on the dotted line, ask your sales consultant about the rights you are purchasing.

If you are purchasing a title deed, lease/licence or shares, enquire whether the property is free and clear of any charges or liens. If there is any doubt about this enquire about the reserve fund, if any, that is automatically allocated for the repayment of existing charges. Is there a third party, such as custodian, trustee or law firm, that holds the funds on your behalf until a clear title is issued in your name? If no third party or escrow account assurance is in force, you will have to decide whether you wish to commit yourself.

The larger developers, such as public companies, rely on their corporate integrity and often do not use the escrow account system. Having said this, most developers, large or small, will provide a blocked account for you if you are sufficiently concerned. You should be prepared to pay a premium for this service, either in the form of price surcharge or loss of any accrued interest as, after all, you are asking him to tie up his property for a period without the income to offset this.

If you are purchasing under a club membership scheme, it is important to find out if the title to the property is registered in a third-party name (custodian, trustee or law firm) and furthermore, if there is an agreement between the developer and the third party showing that the property is unencumbered and *cannot be* encumbered for the lifetime of your membership.

If you determine that the property has not yet been transferred into the third party's name and/or there are still outstanding charges, you should then make sure that there is an agreement allowing the third party to retain a sufficient proportion of your purchase price to cover the acquisition costs. This is quite normal and most agreements provide this protection.

2. Does your resort belong to a recognised exchange organisation? The two leading exchange organisations, II and RCI, have a strict vetting programme before affiliating a timeshare resort. They review the legality of the rights to occupy and they assess the commercial viability of the resort, its location and quality and the facilities and services on site and nearby. But perhaps most importantly, they conduct interviews with the principals of the company to satisfy themselves of their professionalism and integrity.

This affiliation to either II or RCI gives you a reasonable degree of security. As we discussed earlier, there are a number of new exchange companies entering the market place. In instances where your resort is affiliated to one of the new companies, you should enquire as to their vetting policies, how many resorts are affiliated, what is their published data on membership levels, their exchange confirmations and perhaps most important, who are the principals in the company?

If you are in doubt, ask your consultant to show you their resort affiliation certificate or, if this is not available, ask him to allow you to telephone the exchange company in his presence.

3. How many timeshare units are on offer? A project with five units would certainly be more expensive for you in terms of your annual maintenance charge or have more limited on-site facilities and/or services than would the fifty-unit project.

It is said that no timeshare programme becomes efficient unless it has at least ten to fifteen units. Given, say, fifteen units with an average occupancy of one and a half weeks for some fifty weeks sold, the resort will have some 500 owners at the conclusion of its selling cycle. Therefore, the cost of providing an efficient reception, cleaning and maintenance service is spread. If on the other hand, the resort is limited to five units, the same services would cost the purchaser three times as much, as in many cases the same number of staff would be needed.

Most timeshare projects are developed in phases of five or more units. Make sure you find out the final number of units when all phases are complete. If there will be less than ten, I would suggest that you enquire further about the services offered and their estimated charges.

4. Who controls the management company? So far, you have been offered guidelines on how to secure your property for a fixed price and explained the flexibility of the exchange. It is also important to discuss the future charges at the resort and the protection of your interests. In Chapter 4 the resort management services, their operation, the basis of the charges and the owners' associations were outlined. How then should you protect yourself against undue maintenance-charge increases?

You should determine what, if any, rights you have to remove the existing management team and indeed your ability (with the other owners) to contract with another management team should you find that the management services are lacking or becoming too costly.

The majority of timeshare operations allow for owner participation in the association in various forms. The owners' association is sometimes one hundred per cent owned by the timeshare owners. There are exceptions to the rule, as many developers either have an interest in commercial establishments on site or the scheme is mixed with a hotel, whole-ownership units or rental units. As such, however, the developers have an incentive to maintain the quality of the site.

In most cases, there is an agreement with the timeshare owners binding them into a timeshare owners' association which has a constitution and by-laws. The association in turn usually has the authority to appoint the majority of management directors. The owners, therefore, have the authority, if exercised, to hire or fire the management.

How are the management fees calculated? Most projects use a cost plus a ten to fifteen per cent management fee. During the selling cycle, you will find that the maintenance fee may be fixed or pegged to a cost-of-living index for from one to three years and then it is allowed to float to its natural level. Be very careful about fees that are index linked indefinitely. While it provides you with some assurance at the time of purchase, ask yourself (or the developer), who pays the difference if the price index goes up less than the resort's overheads?

Due to the youth of the industry, many developers are still coming to grips with ascertaining the true maintenance cost per year. A resort with no on-site facilities and minimal common areas will certainly cost less to operate than one with tennis courts, swimming pools and substantial landscaping. And what about the units? What will be the wear-and-tear rate? We suspect that we as timeshare owners will take better care of our units than the one-off package holidaymaker but when will it be necessary to refurbish?

Experience indicates that the annual maintenance fees, inclusive of a sinking fund for the replacement of fixtures and fittings, but exclusive of electricity, currently range as indicated below. The difference between the two rates takes into consideration the level of common facilities on site, the standards of luxury and the location.

TABLE 14
EXAMPLES OF WEEKLY MAINTENANCE CHARGES

Size of Unit	Low £	1986 (est.) Mid £	High £
Studio	35	45	60
1 bedroom	50	65	90
2 bedroom	55	78	110
3 bedroom	60	90	120

Does the resort issue its timeshare management accounts to each owner? This is a must, unless the developer has agreed to a fixed or indexed annual maintenance charge and has the financial resources to back it up in cases where the costs come adrift.

What about your assurances of continued quality? Provided the owners have a majority vote, you are secure. If not, satisfy yourself that there is a third-party assurance that the quality of the units and the standards of the resort will be maintained.

In practice, there are, contrary to what most of us would at first believe, very few problems in running a timeshare management company, provided one vital element is understood at the outset. This is service. In reality, the timeshare product, once sold out, is equivalent to a self-catering hotel with full occupancy, whereby each occupant is a part owner. The key to successful management is to treat owners as owners and not as one-off renters.

So, before you purchase, consider what you have seen of the on-site services. Are the staff friendly? Is it a place you would want to return to?

5. Is your resort a member of a national timeshare council? Rapid growth of the industry has brought forward the need for collective action to promote the general interests and at the same time, offer protection to you, the purchaser.

National timeshare associations in Europe operate in France, Italy, Malta, Portugal and the United Kingdom. There are also national associations in Australia, the Bahamas, Canada, South Africa and the United States. These associations range from pure trade to combining both the trade interests and the interests of the consumer.

The British Property Timeshare Association (BPTA) founded in 1981 has been instrumental in fostering other national associations as it firmly believes that the orderly growth of the industry in each country requires collective action. Due to the large number of British purchasers acquiring timeshares outside the United Kingdom, the BPTA recently opened full membership to non-British based operators who are selling to the British market.

The BPTA adheres to stringent vetting requirements similar to those required by the major exchange companies. The association's President is the Earl of Lindsay, whose ancestral home in Scotland, Kilconquhar Castle, is now a leading timeshare resort. Its Chairman is Alex Smith, and Brian L. Wates is Secretary.

The BPTA offers general information on consumer interest and assists developers and marketeers in developing their activities. Members of the association follow a code of ethics, which must be prominently displayed at all times.

BPTA Code of Ethics

1. Members shall be honest and make full disclosure in their dealing with the public and, in particular, with the customers of the timeshare industry. They shall avoid making misleading descriptions, or misrepresentative or extravagant claims with respect to timeshare.

2. Members shall make full and accurate disclosure to customers of all relevant information and, in particular, shall endeavour to make accurate disclosure of maintenance costs and operating costs payable by customers on timeshare projects, including cost of provision for replacement of fixtures and fittings.

3. Members shall encourage all property purchasers to make an on-site inspection of the development.

4. Members shall ensure that developer members shall make suitable financial arrangements so that completion of units in timeshare projects is financially underwritten.

5. Members shall ensure that sales to customers are made upon terms that protect the customer from misuse or loss of monies paid for purchase, hire, or lease of units prior to completion of the legal documents for such acquisition.

6. Members shall provide an option to the purchaser to ensure that, until completion of construction of the units, monies paid by the customer and the customer's title to the unit are held securely under trust, escrow, or similar arrangements.

7. Members shall ensure that timeshare projects are planned, designed, and built in compliance with all applicable laws and regulations.

8. Members shall conduct their timeshare business to such high standards as will ensure first-class service and accommodation at all times.

In October of 1986, the BPTA formally adopted a policy that gives purchasers five working days to cancel their contract of purchase. Membership of the BPTA is restricted so that only those property timeshare developers and marketing companies that can fully satisfy the stringent financial, legal, ethical and quality-control criteria laid down by the association will be accepted.

At BPTA member resorts it is required that your legal documents convey a right of occupancy to the purchaser that cannot be disturbed by prior claims or charges on the property. If in doubt, get your solicitor to contact the developer's solicitor. However, if you have any queries, do not hesitate to contact the BPTA.

Should there happen to be cause for complaint at your resort which you cannot resolve yourself, the BPTA is there to help you. The Secretary will try to intervene in the first instance, but if this fails, then you have recourse to the Consumer Protection Committee through a formal procedure. The CPC is an independent committee and, under its guidelines, the BPTA is obliged to accept its recommendations – which may even include the expulsion of a member.

Consumer Protection Committee (CPC)
The Consumer Protection Committee of the British Property Timeshare Association was formed in December 1982 to protect the interests of the timeshare buyers.

The Chairman is Ronald Coker (Honorary Life President of the Association of Corporate Trustees), and its members are Sir Marcus Fox MBE (at the time of writing, Conservative Member of Parliament for Shipley, Yorkshire), Michael Hanson (Estate Market Correspondent, *Country Life*) and David Hoppitt (Property Correspondent, *The Daily Telegraph*).

Complaints should be accompanied by a filing fee of £20 to cover all administrative costs, which is returnable if the complaint is deemed justifiable. These should be addressed to: The Secretary, British Property Timeshare Association, Westminster Bank Chambers, Market Hill, Sudbury, Suffolk CO10 6EN, tel: 0787 310749, tlx: 987177.

Full particulars of each complaint must be forwarded for entry in the Complaint Book, and must include the following information: date, particulars of aggrieved party, particulars of complainant, brief description of complaint, copies of all supporting documents.

The Secretary will then try to reach an agreement between the complainant and the trader concerned. Failing this, he will try to reach an agreement between the Executive Council of the BPTA and the trader. Should he still be unsuccessful, the file will be presented to the Consumer Protection Committee for adjudication, when a time limit of six months will be imposed for any one case; however, the CPC reserves the right not to review a complaint if it is considered frivolous by majority vote.

The CPC may seek professional advice to help them reach a decision. In all cases their decision will be made known to the complainant in writing and will be certified by the committee's Chairman and Secretary. A copy of each and every decision will be forwarded to the parties in the dispute.

The decision of the CPC, although not legally binding, is final and becomes binding upon the BPTA member where a complaint is upheld. All decisions made by the CPC will be made public in the form of a press release. Needless to say, this particular threat hanging over a member's head makes him most attentive to any consumer complaint filed with the Secretary.

In the case of a non-member, the BPTA uses its 'moral suasion' to seek a solution for the consumer if the complaint is deemed valid.

The committee's recommendations of action are final. It has full authority to sanction, fine or expel a member without further recourse by the member.

In all instances where a consumer complaint is upheld, the council is required to issue a press release to the national press stating its findings.

European Holiday Timeshare Association (EHTA)

Formed in late 1985, EHTA represents a number of British and foreign-based timeshare developers, marketing and service companies representing the industry. The association provides a member vetting process and arbitration procedures in case of disputes between members and their clients. The Secretary

General is Colonel Jeffery Gilhead.

Timeshare Developers' Group (TDG)

Formed in mid 1986, the TDG represents the major UK timeshare companies within the industry. Its members include Barratts, European Ferries, Kenning Atlantic, Aspect/Langdale, McInerney and Wimpey and the two largest timeshare exchange organisations Interval International and Resort Condominiums International.

The companies formed themselves into a group in order to establish a code of conduct and to provide a common platform to promote their commercial interests with various governmental departments in Great Britain and in other countries where they have interests.

Other National Associations

The world industry is now represented by a number of national timeshare associations, all of which are prepared to guide the consumer. Full details of their names and addresses are given in the Useful Addresses section at the end of the book.

Future Legislation

The industry expects a certain degree of future legislation as it becomes more mature. For the moment, the national associations and the two major exchange companies are providing a system of self regulation, but there are a few areas where immediate government legislation would be most helpful.

Due to the hybrid nature of the product, the industry is to a large degree adopting existing legal property documentation as the basis on which to issue occupancy rights. With the exception of France and Portugal, no European government has yet addressed itself to this problem. What is needed is specific national or EEC legislation to create a legal basis for the two classic types of timeshare, that of ownership in perpetuity and that of rights of occupancy which are conveyed for a certain number of years.

It would be most appropriate to see the introduction of certain minimum standards applied, protecting purchaser's monies until they have received their signed documentation. While it is not practical to ask a developer to place the total sales proceeds in escrow prior to the release of the documents, it is certainly practical for the developer to earmark a fixed percentage from each sale to assure the completion of the property acquisition, costs of the fixtures and fittings and the attendant legal costs.

The majority of developers voluntarily undertake to provide this assurance in their existing documentation. However, this is an area that can lead the under-capitalised developer/marketeer to expose the purchaser to an unnecessary risk.

A self-imposed 'cooling-off period' from five to fourteen days would take the sting out of those situations where sales representatives overstep the ethical salesmanship boundary by selling the product to people who genuinely do not need it or cannot afford it.

Conclusion

Do you need to consult your solicitor, accountant or bank manager before you purchase your timeshare? Most people view the purchase of a timeshare like that of purchasing a car, for both are usually visual sales where the documentation is completed on site. There may be occasions, however, when you may not feel totally comfortable with the documentation and you feel that outside advice is needed. It is important, though, that whoever you consult has some understanding of the product. Unless your solicitor, accountant or bank manager understands the product, he may find it difficult to allocate the time to properly vet the documentation unless he asks for a fee. If on the other hand he understands the product, well and good.

If you do run into difficulty at any stage remember, no matter what the consultant says, the final decision to purchase is with you. He will usually understand if you have a serious doubt. In this case, a suggestion would be to contact the developer's solicitor and ask the consultant if you may call your solicitor and have your problems ironed out there and then.

7 General Information

As a timeshare owner you will have the opportunity to enjoy many benefits through your resort and your membership in the exchange company, and from specialist timeshare-orientated service companies. These benefits cover a wide spectrum – travel and exchange, rental, resale and group discounts on a variety of items.

Travel Concessions

Airlines are becoming more interested in the timeshare owner. They particularly like the idea that you travel to and from your resort on the same days each year. This means that if they are able to capture a certain number of families travelling, for example, from London to Malaga or London to Faro on specific days, they will be able to operate back-to-back flights, thus guaranteeing themselves occupied seats, which in turn means passing savings on to the passengers. It only takes some fifty families travelling to and fro on a Saturday to fill up a Boeing 737. Airlines are trying to find a way to attract passengers to take the same flight on the same date for a successive number of years.

Both OSL and Monarch airlines have 'travel clubs' orientated to the timeshare owner. Both companies offer substantial savings on round-trip fares to most European destinations. It will not be too long before many airlines will have travel packages specifically designed for the timeshare owner.

Exchange Company Services

The exchange companies, while primarily offering the exchange service, also offer a wide range of other benefits. As a member of one of these companies, you will obtain advantageous air-travel prices, car-hire discounts, discounts on hotels and cruise liners, and other benefits. It is worthwhile keeping up your membership to the exchange company so that you continue to be eligible for these benefits.

The multinational exchange organisations provide all or some of the member benefits in the Table 15.

TABLE 15
II/RCI MEMBER BENEFITS

	RCI	II
Worldwide annual directory	x	x
European directory	x	x
Periodic magazine:		
RCI Holiday magazine	x	
Traveler magazine		x
Membership card	x	x
Membership newsletter	x	x
Exchange confirmation information		
package		x
Transfer of membership privilege	x	x
Master Membership		x
Flight discounts	x	x
Holiday insurance	x	x
Two-for-one to US	x	
Car-hire discounts	x	x
Cruise discounts		x
Timeshare purchase finance package	x	x

Resort Services

In many instances, resorts will offer a wide range of discounts at selected sporting clubs, golf courses, restaurants, bars and so on in the area. If your resort is a combination of hotel, timeshare and whole ownership with commercial and recreational facilities on site, your club membership will often enable you to use facilities at a discount.

Many resorts also offer an in-house exchange and rental programme. Timesharing lends itself to the movement of groups of people on specific dates each year. This means that we have the advantages of 'bulk buying' which we would not have if we were to strike out on our own each year.

Letting

As discussed earlier, the exchange facility offers you many advantageous facilities. Do not forget, however, that not only can you exchange but you can also rent out or sell your timeshare. This is where the industry is still in its infancy. It is important to understand this before you consider purchasing a timeshare primarily for letting or for its resale investment potential.

Generally speaking, it will only profit you marginally to immediately let for income, as the market will not sufficiently value your unit to make it worthwhile for you, particularly after you have paid a rental commission. Timeshare rentals only become interesting a few years after you have purchased, once you have enjoyed your holidays and benefitted from the cost savings through the increased level of luxury, community facilities and perhaps the exchange system.

Commission rates on rentals reflect the local market conditions. In the United States, Canada and South Africa they are quite high and can be up to forty or fifty per cent of the actual rental value. In Europe they rarely exceed twenty-five per cent. The percentage commission variation is the outcome of factors such as supply and demand, local rental legislation, and corporate objective, namely, subsidised commissions to encourage prospect lead generation to the resort. However, as the industry matures, commissions will seek their natural level.

Most countries where timesharing exists are witnessing the emergence of specialised rental service agencies, either as separate companies, or in conjunction with established travel bureaux. Such firms tend to levy an initial listing charge, sometimes deducted against commission upon sale, and a commission ranging from twenty to fifty per cent, sometimes with a fixed minimum level.

As far as the rental charges are concerned, in Europe these are normally inclusive except for electricity, gas and sometimes water. In Scandinavia many rental prices exclude linens. In the United States and Canada, on-site facilities as well as housekeeping costs are usually billed separately. However, as the units are so luxurious, those who rent at timeshare resorts do tend to get far better value for money than they would elsewhere.

Most resorts offer a rental service for their owners. The British-based Timeshare Bourse offers a European-wide service for owners to list their timeshares for rental through an elaborate electronic system tied in with several travel agents.

Alternatively, the most cost-effective way is to rent the unit out to your friends and thereby save on the rental agent's commission.

Reselling

There are a number of reasons why you may wish to resell your timeshare. Upon reflection, you may decide that the week(s) you bought were not suitable. You may want to purchase additional weeks next to your week(s) when there are none available for sale. You have used your timeshare and the exchange system several times. Perhaps you would prefer to purchase at another resort or buy a larger or smaller unit. In many cases, it becomes necessary to sell due to financial hardship.

Whatever your reason for selling your timeshare, it is important to realise the economics of the resale. As a purchaser you have made a decision to guarantee your future holidays at today's prices plus an annual maintenance fee. The developer, on the other hand, is anxious to sell his unsold weeks as fast as possible in order to realise his profits. Understandably, he may well refuse to assist with your resale as this would directly compete with the sale of his unsold weeks.

Your best bet is to find out who owns the weeks before and after you. It may be likely that they wish to buy. Failing this, enquire if your friends are interested.

The cost of presenting the timeshare concept is quite expensive, often ranging from thirty to forty-five per cent of the sale price. These costs must obviously be included in the purchase price. When adding the marketing costs and sales administration which processes twenty-five or more owners per apartment, we can gain some understanding of why the average timeshare price, when all fifty weeks are added together, often equals approximately three times the retail value of the unit if it was sold on the open market.

Again, the timeshare is a hybrid falling somewhere between owning a second home and the travel package. As suggested before, it is more like a car than anything else. While we may desire to be the first owner of a car and are prepared to pay a premium for this pleasure, we know that as soon as we drive the car out of the showroom it drops in value. Similarly, while we will not lose our asset with the timeshare purchase as we would with a one-off holiday package, we must also realise that the instant resale value of the timeshare will probably be less than the original purchase price when sales commission charges have been deducted.

In fact, industry statistics indicate that if you resell your timeshare on the open market, the price may only reach around sixty-five to seventy-five per cent of the current developer's sales price. This is not necessarily a bad thing. When we consider our savings on holiday costs over a couple of years and include the level of luxury and general facilities enjoyed, most of us would agree that we have had value for our money, even if we achieve a resale price lower than the developer's current sales price – which, it must be remembered, has probably increased by fifteen to thirty per cent in a year.

As the industry matures, a viable resale market will materialise and timeshares will have a proper market value. For the moment, the developer is setting his market price. Most timeshares must be held for three to five years before any resale profit can be made. Unless you are fortunate to purchase at a development where resales are placed into their new sales inventory, you will probably find it difficult for the first few years to sell at a good price.

For the moment, the greatest unresolved problem in the timeshare industry is the creation of a viable resale market, as unfortunately, resales compete with new sales.

Resorts sold out, and those close to that stage, are experiencing about a ten per cent resale level among their owners. However, because the industry is still comparatively young, many promoters have hoped that this rising demand would go away as it constitutes a pressure on their ability to maximise the current values of the remaining unsold units in their projects. However, the promoters who have ignored the demand for resales have often found themselves competing with a secondary source of their own product.

Resale facilities vary greatly in the timeshare world. Some promoters – fortunately only a minority – refuse to do anything about them at all while others say they will only arrange for resales once they are sold out. Others create a smoke screen by offering to buy back at the original purchase price, less the equivalent rental value if the unit has been rented out since the purchase. The net result is that often the owner is not only dissatisfied, but also mistrustful of the management company – knowing full well that his unit will probably then be sold on at its current market value. Another group do accept resales for listing, but subordinate these units by placing a lower sales commission on them, thus lessening their chances of being sold.

In all fairness, a promoter's chief aim is to sell out at the earliest possible date. However, there may be gaps in his listing at given weeks or seasons where resale requests will be the only units available. And in these circumstances it is not at all disadvantageous to him for the resales to be incorporated in the sales programme.

It is important from the owner's standpoint to understand that during the early part of a selling cycle priority must be given to the unsold units because of the negative cash-flow position. One solution to the resales problem is to establish a system whereby they will only be accepted from owners having held their unit(s) for, say, a minimum of three years, but that the company will use its discretion in cases of severe financial hardship.

Should you decide to use a broker, do not be too concerned if he has a large number of resales registered. Many owners automatically list to 'test the waters' so to speak. Secondly, brokers can only provide a cost-effective service to their clients when their listing is sufficiently extensive to enable them to mass market the timeshares. Their interests are to secure the resale at the earliest date as the listing fee will only cover costs and not make a profit. It is a good idea, however, to see if a broker is oversupplied with a particular resort. While large numbers are not in themselves a problem, they could well become a problem if they are bunched around certain weeks and unit sizes.

Commissions on resales vary considerably; however, they are all very high. Developers and marketing companies will normally resell their timeshare for commissions ranging from fifteen to thirty per cent of the resale price.

The Timeshare Bourse is the largest European resales company. The 1986 charge to list one week is £39.50 for a twelve-month period. The TSB provides a full service including handling and distribution of proceeds, the processing of all paperwork and creating a market for the timeshares.

Unlike the stock exchange, the TSB has to attract both buyer and seller. Its function and commission levels are similar to auction houses'. The TSB charges a commission of fifteen per cent less the listing fee for each transaction. It encourages potential purchasers to take a holiday at the resort before completing their purchase. In accordance with the practice of most sellers, the new purchasers, if they complete within thirty days after their holiday, receive a credit for the holiday rent paid for using the timeshare unit.

An alternative is to advertise in the local or national newspapers. If you decide to take this route, be careful, as it can become very expensive.

As a buyer, resales should not be overlooked. Some are discounted up to fifty per cent of the current developer price. This is an excellent opportunity to purchase additional weeks at bargain prices for use as second holidays or to add to your existing timeshare weeks for exchange purposes.

Rules for Letting and Reselling

At the present stage in the growth of the industry, you should not purchase for either immediate rental or resale. Should you need to do so, the following summarises the best ways to go about either.

Priority Level	Method
1	Contact your friends
2	Contact your resort
3	Contact an independent third party such as the Timeshare Bourse
4	Advertise

The Impact on the Local Economy

Timeshare schemes, through a combination of fear of the unknown and ignorance of the product, may sometimes appear to constitute a threat to a local community. There is concern as to how what is seen as a 'hotel-type' operation might settle in a semi-rural or a genuinely residential area.

It is fair to say that a number of timeshare schemes – notably in Hawaii, Florida, Portugal and more recently in Spain – have gone to extremes in their selling techniques. (It has been known for holidaymakers to be approached maybe three times during one single day with various offers to inspect local timeshare schemes.) And of course this 'gives a dog a bad name'.

The professional promoters recognise these excesses and have taken steps to reduce such occurrences in line with the wishes of local residents. A number of local authorities, in areas such as the Algarve in Portugal, Florida in the United States and the state of Queensland in Australia, have introduced either legislation or guidelines to control off-site sales techniques.

In visual terms, timeshare schemes can provide real benefits to the area in which they are located. The physical structure, design, and layout of most timeshare projects are developed to blend in with the local environment. Timeshare appeals to us because it is there, it is visible, it is exciting, and usually within reach of our pockets. As such, the object of a promoter's exercise is to develop his project in such a way that it appeals more to our emotions rather than purely the practical (investment) side, therefore, most timeshare schemes tend to stand out as well-appointed and eye-catching structures.

The profile of the average timeshare owner has emerged as a settled, rather affluent, married couple, half of whom are graduates, and who have one or more children. In short, the ideal next-door neighbours!

The local economy also benefits from timesharing. During the construction cycle, there is of course the local purchasing of building materials, fixtures and furnishings and the employment of local labour to erect the building. Then there is the benefit of employment, with the need for management staff and maintenance personnel. But the true benefits will be derived from the spending power of the timeshare owners.

Let us take a typical timeshare example. Assume a fifty-apartment building which is sold out for fifty weeks of the year. Each family in residence will probably spend about £400 per week excluding the annual maintenance charge. Therefore, the combined spending would be about £1,000,000 per year. Add into this a further £200,000, which reflects a maintenance charge of, say, £80 per unit week. It means the development is putting into the local economy close to £1,200,000 per year.

A further point which is often overlooked is the so-called multiplier effect this has on the local economy. It works like this. Most, if not all, the timeshare owners earn their incomes from outside the local community. Therefore, when they spend their £400 per week on food, entertainment, petrol and so forth and the management spends the maintenance fees, they are bringing money from outside and putting it into the local community. This 'outside' money creates what is known as the multiplier effect, because the opportunity of employment in a community is further increased as there is now more money in circulation than before.

The Tourism Advisory Group's research estimates that the typical timeshare apartment or villa, once sold out, will create a multiplier of seven within the local economy. So for every timeshare apartment or villa built and sold a further seven families will be supported.

If we look back at our example, the fifty-unit building will permit a further 350 families to live in that area.

(*Note* The use of multipliers is not an exact science and therefore these estimates should be considered as generalised data. The multiplier factor is very dependent upon the 'leakage' of money when goods are purchased outside the local economy.)

8 A Brief History of Timesharing

As we now know, timesharing today is international. There are over 1,750 projects existing in at least fifty-five countries worldwide, with close to two million families now owning timeshares.

Once a cottage industry, timesharing has now exchanged its image to one of professionalism. But it still owes a lot to the early pioneers such as Dr Hans Schalch of Switzerland – whom one can possibly call the father of timesharing, the Japan Villa Club Group in Tokyo and Monsieur Louis Poumier of France.

Switzerland

Dr Hans Schalch, a Swiss businessman with a considerable interest in the package holiday field, launched Hapimag from Baar in 1963, a time when he was primarily concerned with providing a regular flow of holiday apartments for his clients, mainly in the city and resort areas of central Europe. His apartment purchases in major cities such as London, Paris and West Berlin gave him further control of a supply of accommodation which he funded by selling shares in Hapimag and allocating a fixed number of points to each share. With the proceeds he acquired further apartments, this time also selling shares and allocating a number of points to each week of the year, according to seasonal demand. The greater the number of shares owned, the higher the priority in obtaining a high-season apartment.

The system worked well. The number of shares was kept in balance with the total points allocated, and a system was set up to preclude substantial shareholders from dominating any particular apartment or time of year.

Dr Schalch never looked back. Hapimag now has well in excess of 40,000 shareholders and close to 2,000 wholly owned apartments covering eleven European countries, including a castle in Scotland. His company has a market value in excess of £100 million, has no debts, and is still growing.

Japan

In 1966 and on the other side of the world a Japanese group of companies based in Tokyo launched the Japan Villa Club of Tokyo after realising it had to come to grips with the holiday needs of its employees. The Japanese have most irregular holiday patterns – a 1981 study indicated that the average annual paid leave amounted to fifteen days and that in addition there were seventeen further days leave for national holidays. These days tended to be split into three shortish periods for New Year, summer and Golden Week (end of April, beginning of May), with the balance being taken one day at a time.

Amazing as it seems, the Japanese group was totally unaware of Dr Schalch's scheme, yet the two systems ran closely parallel. Both started out with individual units. Both subsequently realised that their overheads were out of proportion in relation to the number of apartments in any one given place – which eventually led to their move to purchase entire blocks and sell off where possible any loss-making individual units previously acquired. The Japanese also needed the flexibility to allow for catering for such a casual and unorganised holiday pattern.

Having set up a system to cater for company employees and having found that it worked well, it was not long before the Japan Villa Club started selling shares outside the group and the Japanese timeshare industry was born. This scheme naturally produced a number of rivals within the country, to the extent that Japan is now placed as 'number two timeshare country' – with more than 300 resorts and over 250,000 members.

France

Still 1966 but back in Europe once again, this time with Monsieur Louis Poumier, a director of Les Grands Travaux de Marseilles – a well known construction concern within France. During that year the firm had acquired a large tract of land in the French Hautes Alpes, near a tiny village called St Etienne-en-Devoluy, in order to develop a 5,000 bed, fully integrated ski village – to include ski lifts, bars, restaurants, boutiques, grocery stores and cinemas. The scheme posed some financial problems. It is one thing to buy from plans apartments at beach resorts; it is another at a ski resort, where the success of the *pistes* has yet to be established. A Swiss/Italian operation called Eurotel gave Poumier the answer.

In the early days Italy had had no adequate longterm financing facilities to ensure the viability of its projects. An Italian furniture-making company involved with Eurotel had come up with the answer. Why not construct an apartment block, sell off the apartments by weeks, and then offer to rent them out for holidays on behalf of the owners? It then decided to incorporate sliding doors in the studios to seal off the cooking alcoves and introduce a restaurant; with these modifications it could then go after both the catering and the self-catering markets. The Eurotel chain is now a vast concern within Europe.

M. Poumier had financial considerations that only Eurotel's original thinking could possibly solve, with the one exception that the market was not there for outright sales.

He knew he could fill his resort during Christmas, the Easter and spring-holiday periods, and most weekends – the French have always been very partial to 'le weekend' break. His problem was how to fill the gaps left during the rest of the year when, because of France's fairly rigid holiday patterns, the project would, to all intents and purposes, be empty. He therefore decided to take the Eurotel concept and split his project by time using the Société Civile Immobilière arm of the French Civil Code. The SCI is the legal system which allows shares in a building to be acquired and the rights to its occupancy to be attached to the shares. By issuing various classes of shares, the shareholders then have rights of occupancy at specific times of the year in specific apartments and, on aggregate, own the beneficial interest of the asset. Nearly word perfect for the purpose for which M. Poumier wanted it.

The project was structured so that the high-season periods were sold by the week and the low-season periods by the month. The floating Easter period and the annual school holidays were set specially each year to fit in with the changes in dates and the weeks on either side were floated to accommodate these variations.

Superdevoluy, launched in 1967, was an immediate success.

Generally acknowledged to be the first 'classic' holiday-timeshare scheme anywhere in the world, it divided its apartments into units of time, which were then sold to the public. Hence the origin of the phrase 'holiday timesharing' as we understand it today.

The United States

The following year, 1968, saw the Americans enter the field, completely unaware of what had been happening in Europe and Japan. A group of Washington-based businessmen was considering what to do with a development in Hawaii and decided the only way to make it viable was by timesharing.

The Hawaii Kailana became the first American timeshare scheme, but it was not long before a number of big names such as the Hyatt Corporation and the Playboy Group saw the potential, and the benefits for certain of their developments which were perhaps not showing the returns expected.

During the 1960s there was a boom in apartment building. This turned sour during the early part of the 1970s, mainly due to a backlash against the property developers because of a lack of finance for private development. Although holiday timesharing had made a start in 1968, it was not really until the multi-apartment property bubble burst that the timeshare industry got under way in America.

Even today a great many people think that property or holiday timesharing started in the United States. Of course they can be excused because of the sheer volume of American-style blocks that flooded the market at the time. Americans, too, are always game for new ideas so anything that happened anywhere else in timesharing around the world was more or less overshadowed and overpowered by their enthusiastic endorsement of it. So, from humble and not very happy beginnings, America has emerged as the largest market in this sector of the world leisure industry.

The Rest of the World

During the late '60s and early '70s the fastest actual growth of holiday timesharing took place in Europe. France still led the field, and then other schemes started to appear in Belgium,

Switzerland, Italy and Spain, including the Balearic Islands. Great Britain's first timeshare scheme started up in Scotland in 1975 when Frank Chapman, unaware of the existence of timeshare elsewhere, introduced his 'new' concept to the British and it was not until the '80s that it reached the Canary Islands and Portugal. Malta is still a comparative newcomer, and there is very little as yet to be seen in Greece.

South Africa's first scheme was launched in 1974 and two years later Canada and the Caribbean joined the race. From then on the rest of the free world was anxious to participate and new schemes started to develop in Mexico, South America and Australasia, with Australia proving to be particularly successful. In fact, the whole holiday timeshare industry has gained such momentum that, for those of you who are more adventurous, schemes are now to be found in such exotic places as India, Thailand and Bali.

Conclusions

Those of you interested in the background will agree it is remarkable that a new form of second-home ownership which provides holidays for a lifetime at today's prices should have sprung from property developers' financial misfortunes. With a few exceptions, figures show that holiday timesharing is the fastest growing sector of the world leisure industry. Moreover, forecasters maintain that it will be a good number of years, probably well into the next century, before saturation point is reached.

If you embark on such a purchase, it will be comforting for you to feel you have not backed a loser. Holiday patterns are always changing, which is why the timeshare concept is so good – there is so much flexibility. In this day and age, too, when the emphasis is on leisure, it is also nice to know that the potential for swapping around the world continues to grow.

To illustrate that flexibility and potential to exchange around the world is the unusual story of Gordon Brewster, an Australian grazier from the state of Victoria. In 1979 he had to retire prematurely due to ill health, so he decided to follow the timeshare trail and travel with his wife whilst he recuperated. The couple now own a staggering fifty-two weeks of timeshares in Australia –

forty-eight in Lake Eildon Country Club at the foot of Victoria's Alps, and the remainder at Vacation Village on the Hastings River at Port Macquarie in the state of New South Wales.

The Brewsters' initial attraction to holiday timesharing stemmed from knowing that they could take advantage of the exchange system – in their case RCI – and to date they have traded for time in about 700 of RCI's resorts in thirty-six countries.

The original idea was only to buy three months of timesharing but, having given up farming, they were faced with having to move house and decided instead to put all their money into holiday-timeshare projects. They can now spend their lives just about anywhere in the world they wish – and to prove how flexible the system is, they spent a whole twelve months in the United States staying at resorts into which they had made their exchanges and covering 93,000 kilometres of highway!

9 The Future

Only the surface of the potential market for timeshares has been explored so far. No country except South Africa has penetrated more than three per cent of eligible families. In the United Kingdom, at the end of 1986 there are only about 85,000 owners out of a total population of over fifty million.

Most timeshare resorts at this stage are developed by individual entrepreneurs: we still await the entry of the mainstream property and financial institutions. Having said this, Barratt and Wimpey have emerged as the two dominant British developers in the public sector, with Jack Petchey's Incorporated Investments Ltd in the private sector. The marketing systems are still, on the whole, quite amateurish and consequently quite expensive. A cost that unfortunately is passed on to the consumer.

The major European tour operators including Thomas Cook, TUI, Kuoni, Intasun, American Express and Thomsons have yet to move into the market place, something they will probably be obliged to do in the near future.

In the USA the Holiday Inns and the Marriott group are now very active in the industry. Britain's Barratt building group bought out Frank Chapman's very successful Multi-Ownership and Hotels group in 1982 and has subsequently expanded its operations with a further timeshare resort in England and two on the Costa del Sol, Spain. Wimpey, their arch rival, started with one, and then a second, scheme in the Canary Islands. They have now expanded into Cornwall and the Costa del Sol, with rumours of a new project in London.

European Ferries plc, the Channel shipping group, has introduced timesharing to La Manga, Costa Blanca, Spain, and to the world-famous St Andrews golf course in Scotland.

Club Meditérrannée, the French based world holiday resort chain, recently purchased Clubhotel, the largest timeshare operation in France, boasting an ownership of over 40,000 families.

Where is the industry heading? The timeshare concept is not unique. Computer-leasing firms coined the term when they leased out time to a number of clients. While we do not call it such, is not membership in a golf, squash, tennis or billiard club, timesharing? After all, you are pooling resources to make available something that as an individual you could not afford.

And what about charter flights, the use of hotels and taxis? Timesharing is all around us. It is a system that brings products and services to the mass market which would otherwise only be possible for the privileged few. It could be argued that timesharing is socially desirable, as it is capitalistic communism. It brings to the masses what only capitalists would have previously enjoyed.

The adoption of the sharing of property ownership into the time dimension is a natural extension of optimising the twin objectives of a) property developers seeking an early return on investment and b) the holidaymaker seeking an enhanced lifestyle at a lower annual outlay.

Business Timeshares

Within the leisure industry, timesharing has been primarily orientated to regional holiday areas, but we are now witnessing the beginning of urban timesharing. Projects now exist in London, New Orleans, Las Vegas, San Francisco and Tokyo. The introduction of split weeks and the opportunity to draw down time by the day has enhanced the viability of these schemes. To date, however, all these schemes cater for the holidaymaker rather than the businessperson.

Gazing into a crystal ball, the businessperson's timeshare apartment would be a purpose-built hotel suite with convertible couches or sofabeds that fold into wall cabinets; kitchenettes to prepare breakfast and sandwiches, coffee, tea and drinks; a sophisticated secretarial system with answering services, telex, facsimile and photocopier services. Travelling businesspeople would be able to telex the hotel's secretarial services to make appointments on their behalf for their arrival. The hotel suite would function as an office during the day and a bedroom at night.

The businessperson would have entered the timeshare scheme by purchasing either blocks of seven-day periods, that can be drawn down on one or more days at a time on a first-come-first-served basis, or by purchasing seven-day periods that float within specific quarters of the year. Whether a fast-moving businessperson making quick appointments, or a commercial traveller on the annual buying or selling trip, the timeshare would cater to their needs.

Hoteliers like this sort of programme as they can presell their accommodation and recoup any investment in the space of one to two years, with no further promotional expenses to be incurred. Managing directors like the programme as it has given their executive staff an enhanced travelling lifestyle. Accountants like the programme as they can capitalise it on their books and control, to some degree, the company's costs.

Promoters like the scheme as, with each new hotel participating in the programme, their future sales become that much easier as new purchasers realise they can exchange their time within the participating hotels. And, if all the time is not utilised? Well, there are always the multinational exchange companies, all of which would be glad to exchange one week of time in London, Paris or Rome for a week in Marbella, the Bahamas or Acapulco!

Boat Timeshares

A number of attempts have been made to formalise the timesharing of sail and powered boats. Informal timesharing among friends has been a traditional means of funding yachting. However, no one to date has been very successful in converting informal arrangements into a viable commercial scheme.

Yachts
There are a number of obstacles to successful yacht timesharing. The lifespan of a yacht, even a fibreglass one, is not much beyond fifteen years. The cost of replacing the rigging every three to four years is a major item. When one adds in the marketing cost, the economics tend to be marginal if not unfavourable to the promoter.

Then there is, of course, the question of the competency level of the owners and their commitment to spend the next ten to fifteen years taking their holidays on the same yacht. As one can imagine, it would be difficult to marry yacht timeshare with one of the major exchange companies unless levels of yacht competency were previously established or the yacht was sufficiently large to have its own crew.

Yacht timeshare schemes are currently in existence in the Caribbean, the Mediterranean and Sweden.

Powered Cruisers

In this case, we have two types of timesharing. There are powered cruisers under the direct control of the timeshare user and those under the control of a professional captain. The latter can range in size from single-family cruisers to multiple-family cruisers.

Powered-cruiser timesharing suffers from the same problems as yacht timesharing except that, in most cases, the annual maintenance and refurbishment costs are less. There has been some limited success in this field.

Directors of the Swan Hotel, Streatley-on-Thames near London, set up Swan Timeshare Cruisers in 1981. The combination of the use of governors controlling the speed (and wear and tear) – a requirement of the Thames river authorities – and on-site hotels providing full support facilities, has produced a viable scheme.

A few other operators exist in the Mediterranean. However, as with yacht timeshares, no one to date has found the key to long-term success in this area. Yachts and powered cruisers can only really be used on a co-ownership basis with economical boats for private use and captain-controlled ones for multi-family and corporate use.

Cruise Liners

This is one area that could perhaps become viable, if structured in a proper manner. It could be done with a medium-sized liner operating during the summer months in the Mediterranean and during the winter months in the Caribbean. The timespan of the shares would be ten to fifteen years, and the scheme would be affiliated to one of the major exchange organisations. Owners would purchase on a floating-time basis with certain inter-season controls.

The cruiser would also cater for the normal cruise holidaymaker, but timeshare owners would have certain additional benefits in the form of upgraded cabins and member-only lounges. The marketing strategy would be orientated towards joining a worldwide holiday club with a strong emphasis placed on the exchange opportunities. The itinerary would change each year to ensure that owners who wished to travel at similar times each year would have the opportunity to experience a varied holiday programme.

There is no doubt many of us would enjoy the opportunity to spend a week or two each year visiting the many holiday spots in the Mediterranean and the Caribbean, together with the exciting once-in-a-lifetime opportunity of crossing the Atlantic by sea.

In Conclusion

As the industry matures, there will be a greater integration of timesharing into existing and future resorts. Timesharing is only one sector, although an important one, of the world leisure industry. Timesharing in the future will be an integral part of most resort complexes, and timesharing, second-home ownership, rentals and hotel facilities will exist side by side.

Appendix: Your place in the sun – or is it?

The Timeshare Buyer's Checklist, by the Department of Trade and Industry

Timesharing is buying the right to spend your holiday in your 'own' villa or apartment in the place of your choice for a given number of years. You may be able to swap holiday locations and times with other people in timeshare resorts worldwide.

There are many different types of timeshare property – from major leisure resorts in Spain and Portugal to small holiday cottages in the Lake District. But when buying you need to know how much it will cost and exactly what you are getting. Just imagine – you get a letter inviting you to view a timeshare site. Or you're in the middle of town (or on a sunny beach in Spain) and someone comes up to you and talks about timesharing. Maybe they offer you and your friends a drink or a gift to encourage you to view a timeshare development. What should you do?

Here's our checklist:

★ **Sign nothing** during your first meeting with the salesman, unless you are given a written promise that you have the right to change your mind within a reasonable period of time. Most reputable companies will offer this.

★ **Pay nothing** – not even a small deposit – at that first meeting, unless you're already completely sure you want to go ahead.

★ **Beware** of any pressure put on you to sign at once to obtain a discount or other benefit. The salesman will be saying 'You'll only get the discount if you sign today' to other people tomorrow and the next day . . . and the next day.

★ **Beware** of gifts and prizes which may be designed just to encourage you to visit the site or to buy within a deadline.

★ **Insist** on full details in writing of what you are being offered. A responsible developer will always provide them and they should include:
  - the full price;
  - the type of tenure you will have;
  - how you are to pay for it (deposit, instalments, interest rates, credit);
  - a copy of the contract you are being asked to sign;
  - any other terms and conditions;
  - an indication of what will happen to the property when the timeshare has run its course. Will it be sold and a share of the

proceeds passed to you or will ownership pass to someone else without any payment to you?
  – any maps, plans and property descriptions attached to the contract. If the seller will not let you have these documents to take with you for careful study, walk away at once.
★ **Take your time** considering the offer. Read the contract. Take independent advice. A solicitor will be able to look at the contract and other documents and tell you what you'll be committing yourself to. Think carefully:
  – Can I afford it?
  – Do I like it?
  – Will I use it?
  – Is it going to be worth it to me?
  – If the property is abroad, what about the cost of getting there each year? Will there always be cheap flights?
★ **Ask** about the maintenance charges. They are likely to go up after you have bought, so check what is planned, what the charges include, how the increases are to be decided and by whom. Will you have a say in the management arrangements?
★ **Check** that the resort is affiliated to a reputable exchange organisation. (If not, you may not be able to swap your timeshare.)
★ **Check** that there is an owners' association to represent your interests. Can it dismiss the management company if they fall down on the job?
★ **Don't** think of a timeshare as an investment in the same way as when you buy a house or flat as your permanent home.
★ Be especially careful if you are approached while on holiday. Don't get carried away with the exciting holiday atmosphere and don't sign something which you wouldn't be happy signing at home.
★ **What if things go wrong?**
★ **Don't** try to unravel the tangle on your own. Get advice – from your solicitor, from a Citizens' Advice Bureau, from a Trading Standards Department or a Consumer Advice Centre if there is one where you live. Many reputable timeshare developers belong to trade associations who will also look into disputes (see addresses below).
★ **Remember** – a timeshare property is a long-term purchase and shouldn't be bought lightly. If you sign a legally binding contract, you may be held to it. And if the contract was signed abroad, foreign law may apply and British courts may not be able to help you.
So – use commonsense. Be sure you know what you are buying and can afford it. Then – enjoy those holidays!
NB This DTI publication continues with the addresses of the British Property Timeshare Association, the European Holiday Timeshare Association and the Timeshare Developers Group (see Useful Addresses).

Useful Addresses

Consumer Protection Agencies

British Property Timeshare
Association (BPTA)
The Secretariat
Westminster Bank Chambers
Market Hill
Sudbury
Suffolk CO10 6EN
Tel: (0787) 310749
Tlx: 987177

European Holiday Timeshare
Association (EHTA)
116 Westbourne Grove
London W2 5RU
Tel: (01) 221 9400

Timeshare Developers Group
Communications Group plc
2 Queen Anne's Gate Building
Dartmouth Street
London SW1H 9BP
Tel: (01) 222 7733

Australasian Resort Time-sharing
Council (ARTC)
Suite 514
185 Elizabeth Street
Sydney
New South Wales 2000
Tel: (02) 264 3189
Tlx: AA75003

The Bahamas Time Sharing and
Development Council (BTDC)
PO Box F2058
Freeport
Grand Bahama Island
Bahamas
Tel: (809) 352 8425

and

PO Box N10600
Nassau NP
Bahamas
Tel: (809) 326 2340

National Time Sharing Council of
Canada (NTCC)
Suite 1903
PO Box 12
Toronto Dominion Center
Toronto
Ontario M5K 1AB

Association des Réalisateurs
d'Immobiliers en Propriété
(ARIPSA)
Saisonnière
97 av Victor Hugo
75016 Paris
France

Irish Property Timeshare
Association (IPTA)
Knocktopher Abbey
Knocktopher
County Kilkenny
Ireland
Tel: (056) 28618
Tlx: 28618

Portuguese Timeshare Association
Associacao Nacional Dos
Industriais de Tourismo de
Habitacao Periodica (ANITHAP)
Vale Do Lobo
Centro De Servicos Valverde
8100 Almansil
Portugal
Tel: (089) 9484/5
Tlx: 56877

Central Mediterranean Timeshare
Association (CMTA)
Carmille Dokkiena Street
Luqa
Malta
Tel: 820405

National Timeshare Committee
(NTC)
(Part of South African Property
Owners Association, SAPOA)
503 Carlton Centre
Johannesburg 2001
Republic of South Africa
Tel: (011) 331 2637
Tlx: 87245

National Time-Sharing Council
(NTC)
(Part of American Resort Recrea-
tional Development Ass, ARRDA)
1220 L.Street N.W.
5th Floor
Washington DC 20005
USA
Tel: (202) 3716700
Tlx: 908248

Exchange Companies

Eurex System A.G.
Waldstatter Strasse 9
CH 6002 Lucerne
Switzerland
Tel: (041) 232266
Tlx: 868117

European Passport
Marina Baie des Anges
06270 Villeneuve-Loubet
France
Tel: (093) 200160

Exchange Network
Ocean Springs
PO Box 752
Mississippi 39564
USA

Interval International (II)
European Headquarters
Gilmoora House
57–61 Mortimer Street
London W1N 7TD
Tel: (01) 631 1765
Tlx: 297984

Resort Condominiums
International (RCI) (Europe) Ltd
Parnell House
19–28 Wilton Road
London SW1V 1LW
Tel: (01) 821 6622
Tlx: 28535

Travelex Europe
PO Box 11
Holland
5600 AA Eindhoven
Holland
Tel: (040) 441195

Multi-Location Resort Clubs

Comser International Ltd
(Representing Hapimag with
resorts in eleven European
countries, and planned in
Scotland)
Orantecq House
Fairview Road
Timperley
Cheshire WA15 7AR
Tel: (061 904) 9750

Villa Owners Club
(Representing Holiday Property
Bond with resorts in England and
six European countries)
19–21 High Street
Newmarket
Suffolk CB8LX
Tel: (0638) 660066

Publications: Consumer

Homes Overseas
Homefinders (1915) Ltd
387 City Road
London EC1V 1NA
Tel: (01) 278 9232

Homes and Travel Abroad
Domus Publications Ltd
246/248 Great Portland Street
London W1
Tel: (01) 387 7878

Publications: Legal

International Timesharing
(by James Edmunds)
Services to Lawyers Ltd
197–199 City Road
London EC1V 1JN
Tel: (01) 251 4001

*Practical Timeshare & Group
Ownership*
(by Colin Jenkins)
Butterworths
88 Kingsway
London WC2B 6AV
Tel: (01) 405 6900

Publications: Trade

International Timeshare News
Westminster Bank Chambers
Market Hill
Sudbury
Suffolk CO10 6EN
Tel: (0787) 313424
Tlx: 987177 TAG UK

Resales and Rentals

The Timeshare Bourse
Westminster Bank Chambers
Market Hill
Sudbury
Suffolk CO10 6EN
Tel: (0787) 310755
Tlx: 987177

United Kingdom and Ireland Developments

Allen House
Allen Street
London W8
Tel: (01) 938 1346

Barnham Broom Golf & Country
Club
Barnham Broom
Norwich
Norfolk NR9 4DD
Tel: (060545) 393

Blakeney Timeshare
Blakeney
Nr Holt
Norfolk
Tel: (0263) 740049

Brantridge Park
Balcombe
Haywards Heath
West Sussex
RH17 6JT
Tel: (0444) 400235

Broome Park
Barham
Canterbury
Kent CT4 6QX
Tel: (0227) 831701

Carlton Hotel
East Overcliffe Drive
Bournemouth BH1 3DN
Tel: (0202) 22011

Carvynick Cottages
Summercourt
Newquay
Cornwall TR8 5AF
Tel: (087251) 716

Cherry Orchard Aparthotel
Station Road
Port Erin
Isle of Man
Tel: (0624) 833811

Clowance House
Praze an Beeble
Camborne
Cornwall TR14 0PT
Tel: (0209) 83111

Clovelly Country Club
Woolsery
East Yagland
Bideford
N. Devon
Tel: (02373) 442

Court Barton
South Huish
Nr Kingsbridge
S. Devon TG7 3EH
Tel: (0548) 561919

Coylumbridge Highland Lodges
Club
Coylumbridge
Aviemore
Invernesshire
Scotland PH22 1QN
Tel: (0479) 810673

The Craigendarroch Club
Braemar Road
Ballater
Royal Deeside
Scotland
Tel: (0338) 55558

Dalfaber Golf & Country Club
Aviemore

Scotland
Tel: (0479) 811 244

De Vere Mews
Canning Place
Kensington
London W8
Tel: (01) 491 2677

Devoncourt Hotels
Douglas Avenue
Exmouth
E. Devon
Tel: (0395) 272277

Elmers Court Timeshare & Country
Club
Lymington
Walhampton
Hampshire SO4 8ZB
Tel: (0590) 76011

Fitzpatrick Castle
Killiney
County Dublin
Ireland
Tel: (01) 851533

Forest Hills Trossachs Club
Kinlochard
Aberfoyle
Stirling
Scotland
Tel: (08777) 277

Hillesdon Court
Torquay
Devon
Tel: (0803) 213307

Kilconquhar Castle Estate
Kilconquhar
Elie
Leven
Fife
Scotland KV9 1EZ
Tel: (033) 334 501

Kingswear Park
Dartmouth
Devon
Tel: (08043) 373121

Knocktopher Abbey
Knocktopher
County Kilkenny
Ireland
Tel: (056) 28618

La Grande Mare Country Club
Vazon Bay
Castel
Guernsey
Channel Islands
Tel: (0481) 56809

Lakeland Village
Newby Bridge
Cumbria LA12 8PX
Tel: (0448) 31144

Langdale
Great Langdale
Nr Ambleside
Cumbria LA22 9JD
Tel: (09667) 931

Loch Rannoch Highland Club
Kinloch Rannoch
Perthshire
Scotland
Tel: (08822) 201

Manor Court
Moretonhampstead
Newton Abbot
Devon TQ13 8RF
Tel: (0647) 40859

Marine Quay Club
Cliff Road
Salcombe
S. Devon TQ8 8JH
Tel: (054884) 3554

Melfort Club
Melfort House
Kilmelford by Oban
Argyll PA34 4XD
Scotland
Tel: (08522) 257

St Andrew's Old Course Golf &
Country Club
Fife
Scotland
Tel: (0334) 74371

Connemara Country Club
Leam East Recess
Nr Oughterard
County Galway
Ireland
Tel: (091) 82292

Plas Talgarth Health & Leisure
Club
Pennal
Wales
Tel: (065 475) 631

Quaysider Club
Borrans Road
Waterhead
Ambleside
Cumbria

Renvyle Strand
Renvyle
Connemara
County Galway
Ireland
Tel: (095) 43444

Rhinefield House
Rhinefield Road
Brockenhurst
Hampshire SO42 7QB
Tel: (0590) 22922

Scandinavian Village
Aviemore Centre
Invernesshire
Scotland PH22 1PF
Tel: (0479) 810852

St Davids Vacation Club
29 High Street
St Davids
Dyfed
Wales
Tel: (0437) 720704

St Mellion Golf & Country Club
St Mellion
Nr Saltash
Cornwall
Tel: (0579) 50849

Stouts Hill
Uley
Nr Dursley
Gloucestershire
Tel: (0453) 860321

Sutton Hall
Sutton-Under-Whitestonecliffe
Thirsk
Yorkshire Y07 2P5
Tel: (0845) 597200

Swan Timeshare Cruisers
The Swan Hotel
Streatley-on-Thames
Berkshire RG8 9HR
Tel: (0491) 873737

Taymouth Castle Gardens
Kenmore
Perthshire
Scotland PH15 2HH
Tel: (08873) 205

The Lakelands
Lower Gale
Ambleside
Cumbria
LA22 0BD
Tel: (0966) 33777

The Osborne
Meadfoot Beach
Torquay
Devon TQ1 2LL
Tel: (0803) 213311/22232

The Sloane Gardens Club
3 Sloane Gardens
Sloane Square
London SW1
Tel: (01) 730 0925

Trefrize
Trefrize Estates
Bray Shop
Nr Callington
Cornwall
Tel: (056682) 360

Trenython
Tywardreath
Par
Cornwall
Tel: (072 681) 2572

Tresco
The Tresco Estate
Isles of Scilly
Cornwall
Tel: (0720) 22849

Walton Hall
Walton
Wellesbourne
Warwickshire
Tel: (0789) 842424

Glossary

Accrual RCI term for a credit given to a member to use for an exchange.

Annual Percentage Rate (APR) The true cost of money borrowed, expressed as a percentage per annum.

B-backs A marketing term used to indicate a client who has toured the resort and will 'be back' to purchase on another day.

Bonus weeks A term used by resorts to denote extra weeks which may be drawn upon by owners or non-owners at the resort.

Button up Marketing term used to denote a post-sale review with purchaser to assure that he understands the terms and conditions of the agreement.

Buyer's remorse A term used by marketing companies when a purchaser has changed his mind without a valid reason.

Closing costs Legal fees, title, insurance premiums, service charges etc which are due at time of sale.

Cooling-off period see *Rescission.*

Co-ownership Usually denotes the purchase of weeks of multiples of four or more.

Common areas Areas outside of the dwelling unit such as pool, tennis courts and lands that are owned and used by all owners or members.

Condominium Legal term to designate a building legally subdivided conveying beneficial interests to each apartment owner.

Down payment The amount of immediate payment to secure the contractual right to complete the purchase.

Drop A first-day purchase discount.

Eurex An exchange organisation based in Lucerne, Switzerland.

European Passport An exchange organisation based in Nice, France.

Exchange Network An exchange organisation based in Mississippi, USA.

Exchange programme A facility offering purchasers the option to exchange their time in their unit for another unit in another location. Most programmes allow the owner to exchange different weeks of time.

Fee simple A legal basis to own property, in one's own name, free of any condition, limitations or restrictions.

Five-star resorts II term for resorts that have won an award during the previous year under their five-star award programme.

Fixed time Ownership periods pre-fixed by calendar date each year.

Fixed units Ownership within a specific apartment.

Flexchange II term to denote last-minute exchange of from thirty to seven days in advance of the desired travel dates.

Floating time Ownership periods not restricted by calendar date but possibly restricted by season.

Floating units Ownership within a specific apartment size but not within a specific apartment.

Fractional interests See *Co-ownership.*

Guest certificate A written authority from RCI that allows you to give your confirmed exchange to someone else.

Holiday area code II classication of their holiday areas.

Home owners' association A legally constituted group, consisting of all the owners or timeshare owners of a building, which attends to the management of the building and on-site facilities.

II Interval International – major international exchange organisation based in USA with regional offices throughout the world.

Interval dates The dates of specific timeshare weeks.

Interval 500 II distinguished resort recognition.

Interval ownership See *Timesharing.*

Late exchange RCI term used to denote last-minute exchange of from 30 days to 7 days in advance of the desired travel dates.

Lease A version of right-to-use in which the unit is leased rather than purchased.

Maritime sharing II term referring to exchange aboard yachts and other water vessels where charges other than II's exchange fee may be levied to cover food, provisions and other services.

Maintenance fee The annual fee assessed to owners to cover the cost of maintenance and management of the resort, for only the amount of time they purchased.

Master membership II and Exchange Network term to denote a membership that offers ownership at two or more resorts.

Membership code Numbers allocated by II to individual members at a resort.

Mini vacation (Mini-vac) A one or two night stay at a resort usually designed to give a prospective purchaser an opportunity to visit the resort before purchasing.

Non-disturbance clause A protective clause that conveys to the purchaser occupancy of his timeshare unit regardless of default by the developer or owner(s) of the resort.

Not qualified (NQ) Marketing term to indicate a prospect is not qualified by age, financial position or other reason to purchase.

Occupancy limit Maximum number of people who may occupy unit for exchange purposes.

OPC Off-premise consultants, off-site property canvassers, off-site personal contacts – individuals who introduce the timeshare concept to prospective clients outside the resort.

Quarter share – the purchase of one quarter interest in the unit.

RCI Resort Condominiums International – Major exchange organisation based in USA with regional offices throughout the world.

Referral Marketing term used to denote an owner who 'refers' a friend or associate as a potential purchaser to the resort.

Reload Marketing term used to denote an owner who purchases additional week(s) at a resort.

Rescission That period of time following the sale during which a buyer can change his mind, cancel the purchase agreement and get a refund of funds paid on deposit. The period varies by country and by resort.

Resort code II term used to denote a specific II-affiliated resort.

Resort sequence II term: the numerical sequence of resorts according to holiday area codes within twelve main sections.

Space availability code RCI term to denote probability of obtaining an exchange into a particular resort.

Space bank RCI term to denote usage demand patterns.

Split weeks A one-week period divided into two parts, such as Thursday to Sunday or Monday to Wednesday.

Supplementary week RCI term for a spare week made available by a resort which can be used by a member. These weeks may not be accrued.

Timeshare Bourse (TSB) A rental and resale organisation based in England.

Time division RCI term to denote usage demand patterns: red = greatest demand, white = average demand, blue = lesser demand.

Timesharing The purchase of rights of occupancy, usually in multiples of one week for a successive number of years. The rights may be either for a fixed time or in perpetuity and may or may not carry residual interests in the asset value.

Title insurance An insurance policy that agrees to defend the status of the title to the unit week(s).

Tour A term used to denote showing a prospect around the resort with the express intention of asking him to purchase.

Travelex An exchange organisation based in Eindhoven, Holland.

Two for one (2 for 1) RCI term whereby for a limited time, European owners at European RCI-affiliated resorts may exchange one week in their resort for two weeks in a North American resort.

Unit return notice An RCI term denoting a written notification from RCI returning to their member their deposited time as it has not been allocated to another member.

Ups see *Tour.*

Acknowledgements

My primary praise must go to Ger, my wife, who encouraged me to write the book, and prepared the final text of the manuscript for submission.

I would like to acknowledge and thank Marianne Castiglione for her assistance in drafting out a number of chapters during its early development.

My hand goes out to both Ronald Haylock, MD of RCI Europe Ltd and to Edward Davies, MD of Interval International, the two principal timeshare organisations, who were kind enough to wade through the text and provide me with constructive criticism on its contents and approach.

I would like to extend my personal appreciation to Ian Rickson, Planning Research Manager of the British Tourist Authority (English Tourist Board Research Services) who provided me with invaluable advice on its editorial content; to Tony Hepworth of Javafame for the use of his computer services; to Professor Richard Ragatz whose statistics were invaluable and to many friends within the industry who supported me with information and their candid comments.

Thank you one and all.

Index